Copyright © Bernard Allen 2003

ISBN 0 9547124 0 4

First published in Great Britain in 2003 by
Steaming Ltd
51 Truman Drive
St Leonards on Sea
East Sussex
TN37 7TH

A CIP catalogue record for this book is available from the British Library

Printed in Great Britain by Impact Designs, St Leonards on Sea, East Sussex

155.48

Changing Minds

"The greatest discovery is that a human being can alter his life by altering his attitudes of mind."

William James

Contents

Introduction

"The most common of all follies is to believe passionately in the palpably not true. It is the chief occupation of mankind."

H. L. Mencken.

Most people have theories about why people behave the way they do. Many of the common phrases which permeate our language expose assumptions which are rooted in outdated ideas. People still talk about 'winning hearts' even though we have known for some time that emotions are rooted firmly in the brain. They talk about 'letting off steam' although hydraulic models of emotion have long been proved to be false.

Recent discoveries about the brain and advances in evolutionary biology are challenging this view. We now know that the thoughts, plans and strategies which enable humans to pursue long term goals are generated by the more recently developed structures at the front of the brain. We also know that this part of the brain can suppress ideas being generated by other areas which are concerned with more immediate needs. Although the frontal lobes of the cortex are a more recent development, we are beginning to see that emotions were not left behind in the evolutionary process. The mind and brain adapted and evolved in tandem, with emotions playing a central role in cognition. It no longer makes any sense to treat thinking, emotions and behaviour separately. Emotions are an integral part of thinking and behaving. The way we feel affects the way we think and behave. The way we think and behave affects the way we feel.

The advanced structures at the front of the brain do not suppress emotions; they use emotions to suppress ideas from other parts of the brain. Emotions are used to set priorities by the most advanced structures of the brain. Emotions are an integral part of the processes which store important memories. It is the emotions which tell us what is important.
Emotions are the mechanisms by which different areas of the brain fight for control when the ideas they generate conflict. This internal mental conflict which involves the emotions produces physiological changes which can be measured.

It has been known for some time that people suffering from stress may develop health problems, such as heart disease. Now we are beginning to understand the processes involved. Internal conflicts change our mood and there is also evidence that the emotional state influences the way that people think.

Chapter 1 - Thinking

"The seat of the soul and the control of voluntary movement – in fact, of nervous functions in general – are to be sought in the heart. The brain is an organ of minor importance."

Aristotle

According to some estimates, over 95% of what we know about the workings of the human brain was discovered in the past ten years. One reason for the acceleration in knowledge was the discovery of Magnetic Resonance Imaging scanners, which allowed scientists to watch live brains, and observe which bits were active when people were engaged in mental activities. The result has been a revolution in our understanding of psychology which has caused scientists to revise many of their ideas about human behaviour.

The brain is not a singular mechanism which exhibits some unitary quality called intelligence. It is a group of mechanisms or systems, which evolved to accomplish a range of specialised mental tasks. Sometimes these work together but at other times they seem to be competing like two pilots trying to fly the same aircraft.

For good safety reasons the airline industry has developed protocols to avoid squabbles on the flight deck. The brain has also evolved mechanisms to resolve internal disputes and maintain the illusion that there is only one pilot. However, evidence is growing that there is more than one person in our brain. It is when there is confusion over who is in control that problems arise.

All living things are designed to reproduce the DNA which is carried in their genes. According to evolutionary theory that is the ultimate purpose of all behaviour throughout the animal kingdom, but what really drives the behaviour of individual human beings is a combination of urges and tendencies which the DNA has programmed into them. The overall effect of these urges and tendencies over a long period of time has been to successfully reproduce the 99.9% of DNA which all human beings currently share, otherwise we would not be here.

However, evolution is a very slow process. Innate behaviours evolved to give the carriers of those genes the best chance at survival in the natural habitat of hominids living tens of thousands of years ago. The world has changed dramatically since then, but the DNA in our genes has not. Our innate urges and tendencies are not designed for the modern world, and some of them work against the interests of individuals living in the complex, unnatural environments which human beings have created for themselves. For example, we evolved a tendency to prefer sweet, fatty foods because they enabled our hunter-gatherer ancestors to identify rich sources of nutriment. In the modern world those same tendencies cause us to choose unhealthy foods and miss out on nutriments we need.

We also inherited an innate tendency towards 'healthy' appetites. It made sense for our ancestors to binge and store fat when food was in abundance, because most of the time food was scarce. But in the modern western world, food shortages never come, so most people are overweight all the time and suffer ill health as a result.

A whole range of other 'natural' urges and tendencies cause individual human beings to act in ways which prevent them from fulfilling their ultimate purpose. For example, people use contraception or choose to have same sex relationships. They kill themselves and their children in deliberate acts of cruel vengeance. They take dangerous risks in order to get a thrill, or adopt dangerous lifestyles in the pursuit of immediate pleasure by abusing drink and drugs.

It has become fashionable in parts of western society to equate 'natural' with 'good'. 'Natural' foods and medicines are assumed to be healthy whereas 'artificial' additives are believed to be bad, in spite of the fact that the natural world is full of poisons and carcinogens. Similarly some philosophical movements equated 'natural' behaviour with goodness. The concept of the noble savage was based on the myth that all the ills of humanity result from modern culture and if we could get back to 'natural' behaviour, people would be happy and peaceful. The harsh reality is that at one time or another 'natural' behaviour has included bullying, aggression, violence and indiscriminate rape in almost every civilization studied.

As these are the norm, rather than the exception, perhaps we should take a closer look at what passes for 'natural' behaviour. The DNA which makes up modern Scandinavians, who are generally regarded as peaceful people, is the same DNA which drove the Viking Berserkers to rape and plunder. In recent times we have seen peaceful communities in Ireland, the Balkans, Central Africa and many other regions of the world disintegrate into horrific violence. People like us commit atrocities. Perhaps we should take a closer look at how it is that some people learn not to behave unsociably. We like to think that we already know what drives our own behaviour, but evolutionary psychology is teaching us that we are unaware of many of our own psychological processes. In many respects we are no more aware of the operations of our own brains than we are of other organs of the body.

Sub-conscious Habitual Programmes

The kidneys, liver, heart and other organs respond to the various demands being made on them but we are not conscious of the processes. When foreign bacteria invade our bodies they set off an alarm system which results in the manufacture of armies of white blood cells in the bone marrow. These are sent into the bloodstream to do battle with the invaders, yet we are completely unaware of all the drama. If the white cells win a comprehensive victory, which happily for us is the outcome most of the time, the carnage is all cleared away and the body gets back to normal leaving us none the wiser.

Even when the body comes under serious attack, flooded with toxins and the corpses of dead cells, we are scarcely aware of what it going on inside us. We may feel a bit under the weather but continue going about our normal business and wake up the next day feeling fine again. A lot can happen without us being aware of it, even our own behaviour.

When our patellar reflex is checked by the doctor, a light tap on the knee with a rubber hammer causes the knee to jerk up before we are even aware that it has happened. The term 'knee jerk reaction' is commonly used to describe a number of automatic responses. The reason why we are not conscious of the knee jerk response, until after it has happened, is that the decision is not taken by the brain at all – the message never gets that far. The tap on the knee triggers an automatic response at the base of the spinal cord which immediately returns an instruction to the muscles. It saves time.

The knee jerk response does not involve the brain at all, but we are no more aware of decision making processes which do. Extremely complex mental feats can be accomplished subconsciously. We have no more privileged access to the activity in our own brains than we do to the activity in the brains of other people. We only get to see the results.

Catching a ball is a complicated task. Task analysis is the term used for breaking a complex task into smaller components. Catching a ball involves recognising the ball, by decoding the complex interference patters in beams of light bouncing off the ball's surface. This information is stored and compared, millisecond by millisecond, with previously stored patterns to allow the brain to calculate the velocity and likely projectory of the ball. At the same time as all these calculations are going on, other parts of the brain work to adjust the muscles in the eye to keep the ball in focus. The brain coordinates body, hand and eye movement to ensure that the hand will be exactly where the calculations suggest the ball will land. We are nowhere near designing a machine which could accomplish this task, yet all this happens in the blink of an eye without us being consciously aware of any of it. It is entirely subconscious and a five year old child can do it.

In fact, a five month old dog can do it. Many other animals display feats of mental and physical coordination which are beyond our capability. Seals balance balls on their noses; bats calculate the position of objects by decoding echoes from the bursts of sound they emit, and do it so accurately they can avoid piano wire in the dark. Pigeons and salmon can navigate over thousands of miles and find their way home, but it is a mistake to believe that consciousness is necessary for such complicated brain work.

In fact as we become more practised at performing mental feats, we seem to become less conscious rather than more so. With mental activities, just as with physical skills, the more practised we become the less aware we are of what we are doing. That is why practised drivers can daydream for miles, whereas learner drivers need every bit of their conscious mind focused on the mechanics of changing gear and letting out the clutch. Habitual thinking demands much less mental effort than manual thinking. Learner drivers suffer heightened consciousness during their one hour lesson and are exhausted at the end of it. Experienced drivers sometimes set off for the shops thinking about something entirely different, and accidentally drive to work instead.

It follows from this that children, who are learning new things all the time, may be more conscious than adults who are involved in familiar routines. The more practised we become the less we are aware. Some people daydream most of the time.

Innate Similarities

We are discovering that much more of our thinking is automatic and instinctive than was previously thought. For example, people from every culture ever studied recognise the same facial expressions and know what they mean. When people describe their own behaviour they sometimes say that they acted without thinking. The reality is that they were thinking, but it was habitual thinking which is subconscious and goes on in the background. Some patterns of habitual thinking come naturally and seem to be innate. Identical twins, who were separated at birth and raised apart, still show remarkable similarities in a wide range of behavioural traits as adults. The best predictor for schizophrenia and virtually every cognitive and behavioural disorder is to have an identical twin with the condition. This is irrespective of the environment in which the person was raised. Dyslexia, language impairment, left handedness, mental illness, obsessive compulsive disorders and sexual orientation are just a few of the many conditions which run in families and are more likely to occur in identical rather than fraternal twins. Autistic spectrum disorders also seem to have a substantial innate component. There appears to be another innate mechanism in the brain which equips humans to understand other humans, to empathise with their feelings and understand their motivations and behaviour. Autism results from disruption to this innate mechanism and this condition also seems to run in families.

Yet while it is true that twins raised separately show similarities, even those raised together are far from identical in intellect, personality or behaviour. Identical genes do not produce identical people, a fact which does not seem to have been fully appreciated by the more excited proponents of human cloning. Human behaviour is influenced by innate characteristics, family upbringing and other environmental factors. In highly politicised academic institutions in the latter part of the 20th Century much effort was wasted as views about the causes of behaviour became polarised. The debate over whether behaviour is inherited or learned is largely sterile. In the 1970s university psychology departments were obsessed with the Jensen controversy. Jensen (1972) had revived an old debate about whether or not intelligence is inherited. This generated a fear that any discussion about inherited genetic differences could be used to justify racism, sexism and oppression.

These days people are less obsessed with the narrow concept of 'IQ' and more aware of the wider range of human talents and qualities. The human genome was first mapped in 2001 and what is striking is how similar all human beings are. Professor Marcus Feldman of Stanford University reported in the Journal of Science, December 2002, that Human DNA is 99.9% identical. Of the tiny 0.1% variation, 0.094% is amongst individuals from the same population compared with a miniscule 0.006% variation between average individuals from different populations. In short there is not much evidence of any significant genetic differences between races.

Summarising research which has been conducted over nearly half a century and replicated in many countries, Eric Turkhiemer (2000) concluded that there are three laws of genetics:

1. All human behavioural traits can be inherited
2. The effect of being raised in the same family is less than the effect of the genes
3. Most of the variation in behavioural traits between people cannot be accounted for either by the genes or the family

Regardless of the influences of genes or parenting, the evidence suggests that most of the differences between individuals result from other influences in the environment they experience.

What is becoming increasingly clear, as the results of Magnetic Resonance Imaging experiments are published, is that there are significant differences between women's and men's brains, which should come as no surprise to anyone other than radical behavioural psychologists and social scientists. Men and women use different parts of the brain to find their way around. In an experiment reported by Dr Matthias Riepe at the University of Ulm in Germany, men and women were given the task of negotiating their way out of a virtual maze on a computer. MRA scanning of the brain showed that the men, who were much quicker than the women, actually used different parts of the brain to accomplish the task. Unfortunately for males, that is where the good news stops. Women seem to be better equipped in a range of areas. They are better at picking up the subtle signals which show when somebody is upset, whereas men are repeatedly taken by surprise when women burst into tears 'without warning.' What has been called 'female intuition' is more accurately described as a set of innate perceptual skills.

At rest, men's brains are only 30% active whereas females are 90% active. Evidence of differences in the mental capacities of the sexes is not new. It was just more difficult to discuss in the political climate which governed some universities at the end of the 20th century, where dogma became more important than evidence. It has long been known that girls start speaking earlier than boys/ On average three year old girls have twice the vocabulary of three year old boys./Men are four times more likely to suffer speech loss following left temporal lobe damage, whereas women with damage in the same area continue to speak. The reason is that women use more of the brain, and different parts of the brain, for speech and language. There may be some truth in the observation that men aren't very good at listening. Men have fewer connections between the right and left hemispheres of the brain.

Research at the Indiana University School of Medicine, presented at the Radiological Society of North America's annual meeting (2000), showed that men only use one half of their brain when they are listening, whereas women use both sides. Woman really can speak and listen at the same time. Men seem to focus on one thing at a time. The observation that men tend not to go to the toilet together to share information may reflect more significant differences about the way they think and communicate. Few areas of psychology have generated so much popular interest in such a short time as the concept of Emotional Intelligence. The term first appeared in 1990 when Peter Salovey of Yale and John Mayer of the University of New Hampshire used it in a paper to describe their attempts to measure human qualities, such as empathy, which were ignored by traditional intelligence tests.

Five years later the concept became firmly associated with the name of Daniel Goleman, a writer with The New York Times, who used the Salovey and Mayer research as the basis for his best-selling books and a successful management consultancy.

Since 1995 the term has been used in popular books, newspapers and magazines to describe several different things. In his book, 'Emotional Intelligence: Why it can matter more than IQ' (1995), Daniel Goleman claimed that his measures of EQ would turn out to be twice as important as IQ. These ideas seem to have been accepted uncritically by some of the media, but the authors of the original research are more circumspect. Mayer et al (2001) stated that "in spite of the claims of popular authors, we do not believe that emotional intelligence will prove to be twice as important as analytic intelligence in predicting success."

Research from Stanford University, reported in the Journal Proceedings of the National Academy of Sciences (July 2002), showed that the sexes use different neural networks to process emotional events. Women use many more areas of the brain to process information with an emotional component than men. Women use different neural circuits and involve much more of the brain when processing information with an emotional content. Women produce memories of greater emotional intensity than men, and they recall emotional events better and quicker than men. Evolution may have protected males from the implications of their own violence by blunting their emotional responses. Anger seems to be the only human emotion which affects males more strongly than females and it is linked to Androgens, the male hormones which regulate aggression and sex. Males show a different physiological reaction when they are faced by challenge and stress, responding more quickly and more aggressively than females. But it affects their thinking too. Unlike females, males have Androgen receptors distributed throughout the entire brain. Male brains appear to be designed to link all their thinking to sex and violence!

Automatic Programmes Which Drive Behaviour

Many young animals seem to have learning mechanisms which enable their brains to be automatically programmed. These mechanisms allow learning to take place relatively quickly and effortlessly, rather like a self-extracting computer programme, but they can only be used once. These innate self-extracting learning programmes are automatically installed at a specific stage in the animal's development. Once the learning is completed, they are switched off again.

For example, newborn ducks have an innate learning mechanism which enables them to learn to recognise their own mother. It is called imprinting. They only need to learn to recognise one mother, so the learning mechanism is turned off once they have imprinted. The psychologist Otto Tinbergen demonstrated the limitations of this inflexible system. If the first thing a newly hatched duckling happens to see is a bucket, it will imprint on that and believe the bucket to be its mother for ever more.

Nightingales in Berkley Square have a similar learning mechanism which enables them to learn their territorial song. The young birds hear the song of their father and replicate it exactly. But they can only ever learn one song. Once the song is learned the module is switched off, and they can never learn to sing another.

Humans have similar automated programmes, one of which enables them to learn a language. At around the age of three, a programme switches on enabling children to learn the language they hear around them. Most children accomplish this effortlessly at an astonishing rate. They do not need to learn the rules, because basic grammatical rules are already built into the programme. In fact children impose grammatical rules, if they are absent in the language they hear. It was the children of slaves, thrown together without a common language, who imposed innate rules of grammar upon pidgin English to create Creole languages. Pinker (1994) also describes how the signed languages of the deaf were created by children who imposed grammatical rules upon simple signalling systems. By the age of six, the average child will have learned a vocabulary of around 60 000 words, an average of one completely new word every 90 minutes of consciousness, seven days a week, 365 days a year. This is an impressive feat by any measure. Children, who are exposed to more than one language during the period in which the language programme is turned on, can learn more than one language, apparently effortlessly. Sadly the module switches off just before puberty and from then on language learning becomes much more difficult, because humans have to switch to a different learning mechanism.

Inexplicably, schools wait until the language programme is switched off before starting to teach foreign languages. Nobody who learns a language in adulthood attains the fluency of those who learned while the innate programme was still turned on. The reason is that they have to use a completely different learning mechanism.

Although there is an innate programme for learning spoken language, there is no innate programme for learning reading or writing. Exposing children to language will result in them learning to communicate without effort, but exposing children to books does not result in them learning to read and write. This lesson was learned the hard way by children who suffered from the confusion of those educators during the latter part of the last century who confused innate language mechanisms with artificial recording systems.

Reading, writing and basic mathematics are all combinatory skills, so they must be taught and learned in the right order if they are to make sense. We begin with simple concrete operations and work up towards abstract ideas. In order to become skilled, children need to work hard, practising until the skills become automated.

There is no innate learning programme to help humans to appreciate big numbers, mathematics, probability, acceleration or modern social structures. These are all modern constructs, and there has been no time for evolution to keep up with the rapid advances in human culture and science.

It is when we have no innate programme, or a prepared habitual response, that we become conscious. Conscious thinking is much harder work and it is through conscious thinking that human beings have proved to be so adaptable. They have also learned to short circuit the innate urges designed into them for the purpose of replicating DNA. Short circuiting these natural urges to generate pleasure is what human beings spend most of there time doing. It is also what generates problem behaviour.

Pleasure Seeking

Amoebas are simple, single celled creatures which move towards certain stimuli and away from others. We might deduce from their behaviour that they find some stimuli pleasurable and others uncomfortable, but they have no equipment for feeling. Amoebas spend the majority of their time feeding, reproducing or conserving energy. They do not have much time for hobbies or interests.

Many human beings, on the other hand, are able to meet their basic needs with time to spare. This has led to the development of a range of recreational activities which involve pleasure seeking.

We have learned to manipulate the taste for sweet and fatty foods, which in the past guided us towards rich sources of nutriment, by producing artificially processed sweet and fatty foods for our enjoyment.

The sex urge, which in the past drove us to replicate our genes, is artificially manipulated by a vast recreational sex industry which has little to do with procreation.

Innate human urges towards aggression and violence, which in the past drove humans to wipe out their competitors in order to protect their families, is artificially manipulated through sport and games. Each Saturday, the football terraces are packed with people enjoying metaphorical warfare in which nobody really gets killed.

These are all examples of ways humans manipulate pleasure from their innate urges. They may not be aware of it, but everything human beings choose to do in their free time involves manipulating some innate urge for pleasure, be it playing a slot machine in the pub, visiting a garden centre or reading poetry.

Just as the amoeba is innately programmed to move towards certain stimuli and away from others, so human beings are innately drawn towards particular features of the environment. Over the past ten years evolutionary biologists have provided an insight into the sort of environment human beings were designed to inhabit.

The technique is called reverse engineering. According to evolutionary theory, the reason a pattern of behaviour survives is that it enabled the creature's ancestors to survive. They look at how people actually behave and try to work out what function that sort of behaviour might have served in the past. This approach not only enables us to understand behaviour, it also gives an insight into how we can make people feel more comfortable.

For example, it makes sense to acknowledge the sorts of environment which subconsciously attract people in order to create environments in which human beings feel comfortable. This has been described as 'milieu therapy.'

Evolutionary biology also helps us to understand our own behaviour. Powerful emotional responses, such as a fear of heights or snakes, occur in many animals and make adaptive sense. The innate feeling of disgust most people experience at exposure to maggots, vomit, excrement and other people's spit also make evolutionary sense. They are a protection against sources of contamination. Our own spit only becomes disgusting the moment it has left our mouths, and then very few people want to put it back.

A morbid fascination with disasters and other people's misfortune can be understood in the same way. There are evolutionary advantages in a creature having the innate urge to learn more about the calamities which befall their fellows. It may help them to avoid the same fate.

Sometimes people have conflicting habitual responses. Normal people experience mixed emotions when they come across an accident. They experience fear and revulsion, which functions to protect them by urging them away from danger, but at the same time they experience opposing feelings; a 'morbid curiosity' to go nearer and find out more.

This is why the media show us disasters and why we choose to watch disaster movies; we have an innate fascination for such images. Some people find a different, perverse short cut to pleasure which uses this emotional system. They cause other people to experience discomfort and enjoy watching the results.

Fear is also very closely linked to humour, so much so that it could almost be considered to be part of the same emotion. Many of the things that frighten us are also the things that make us laugh. We laugh when we are nervous, and the same part of the brain is involved when we experience fear and humour. Humour is linked to aggression and violence.

A form of humour which appears in all human cultures is 'slap stick,' and the name says it all. People get slapped, hit or hurt and we laugh at them. One of the most popular shows on television is one in which people send videos of accidents happening to their friends and family. The audience laughs at old people falling over, people falling off ladders and children falling off their bikes. But they are repeatedly reassured that nobody was seriously injured.

Other forms of humour involve people being humiliated or made to look stupid. Most jokes involve a story which deliberately misleads the audience. The line which makes the audience laugh is the one that lets them know they have been fooled. Tellingly it is called the 'punch line'. Observational humour describes common human behaviour, which the audience identifies with, in a way that makes it appear embarrassing and foolish. People are anxious that the joke might be on them and relieved to laugh at other people instead.

The noise we make is very similar to a sound made by young chimps when they indulge in ritual play. They bear their teeth and make a sound like, 'hee, hee, hee' as they make playful attacks. The noise and the facial expressions signal that it is not a real attack and nobody is really going to get hurt.

Humour in social situations often involves a ritual interplay of teasing; mock attacks accompanied by the sound which signals it is not a real attack. This teasing can actually serve another social purpose. Many social gatherings consist of people from a variety of backgrounds, and in any social group there are usually differences in status. If people are going to behave as friends in these social situations, they need to put these differences aside temporarily. One way to do this is by engaging in humorous banter. This is particularly evident in groups of men. Socially skilled, high status people allow themselves to be teased and even make self-depreciating jokes to temporarily reduce their status, so that they can interact as equals. Of course they are completely unaware of these processes. Humour can also be used to mask genuine attacks on a person's status. Comedians often use material which is designed to reduce the status of powerful people. In social groups the pecking order can be tested and maintained through humorous banter.

Most social animals seem to have innate mechanisms which regulate status and enable them to know where they stand in the social group. In many animals the 'pecking order' is continually negotiated through play fighting, which may escalate into something more serious. When animals are clear about their relative position in the 'pecking order' they do not need to negotiate or challenge each other. They indulge in ritual behaviour which reinforces their mutual appreciation of their relative status. These innate tendencies to displays of dominance and subservience may explain the mechanisms by which bullying becomes a habitual form of behaviour for some people. It may also explain some of the behaviour exhibited by 'natural victims'. People can get pleasure in strange ways. For example, high status politicians and businessmen have been discovered paying good money to be humiliated and dominated by prostitutes.

The innate mental mechanism which enables humans to understand other people creates feelings of empathy. When people observe something happening to another person they actually experience what they imagine the other person is feeling. Humans have learned to short circuit this automatic response by creating fictional people and stories in books, films and videos. Hollywood provides fictional people, experiencing fictional events which stimulate counterfeit emotions and allow people to manipulate their own feelings. They even enjoy being reduced to tears. Crying stimulates endorphins, which are linked to pleasure and some people deliberately choose to watch 'weepy' films. Those with autistic spectrum disorder who are not equipped with the innate social learning programme just do not get it.

People throughout history have been emotionally affected by music, poetry, dance and painting. The arts feature in every human culture. They are evidence of the way humans have learned to short circuit their innate brain mechanisms to get pleasure. Just asking a person to read a short statement relating a positive experience can improve their mood. Having recognised the power of books, videos and music to change people's mental state, it makes sense to put some effort into selecting what is made available.

Not all the forms of mood altering entertainment, created to play on innate urges, are beneficial. Nor do they all result in positive mood change. People may be drawn towards them but horror and pornographic films involving graphic scenes of violence do not have the same beneficial mood enhancing effects as happy films or comedies. Those with a duty of care should give some thought to what they make available if they want to exert influence on the emotional climate.

Some people use background music to influence mood. Music is processed by the right hemisphere of the brain, so it does not interfere with the parts of the brain dealing with other activities such as language or maths. Scented candles and incense sticks are claimed to promote particular moods. Experimentation will show what works with particular individuals and what does not. Once moods have been induced, they generalise to affect a person's whole perception of their world. People who were given questionnaires after having a mood artificially induced were more positive about everything, including their work and personal relationships.

The evidence that human beings can manipulate their emotions is everywhere. It is what human beings spend most of their time doing.

Habitual Thinking

In addition to the built-in programmes and the self-extracting innate programmes, human beings benefit from another type of learning. It is called thinking. This learning mechanism is slow, it can only do one thing at a time and it makes high demands on resources. When this learning mechanism is in operation it feels like hard work. But thinking allows much greater flexibility to a creature that can do it, because the same basic rules can be applied to many different sorts of task.

The downside is that when this form of conscious learning is taking place it uses up so much of the available mental resources that the animal is barely able to do anything else. This can make the learning animal vulnerable, which may be one reason why human children are protected for so long.

However, once a task has been learned, whether it is mental or physical, it can be rendered into a sub-conscious habitual pattern which works automatically and reduces the demands on mental resources. Gradually, as children grow up they build up a repertoire of habitual responses. The more of these sub-conscious habitual routines we can develop, the more efficient we become and the less mental effort we have to put into thinking. Just as physical skills can be learned and automated through effort and practice, so can thinking skills. By changing the way we habitually think and behave, we can also change the way we habitually feel. There are good reasons why it is worth making the effort, both for ourselves and those who share our company.

Rendering Habitual Learning

The boundaries between innate behaviour, automatic learning and conscious learning are blurred around the edges. As children grow they pick up mannerism, accents, social behaviour and opinions from a range of sources without being aware of it.

Thousands of years ago Ovid observed that, 'Habits turn into character.' For example, most adults have a signature. For many it is a defining icon of their individuality, used to identify them on documents and credit cards. People write their signature automatically, without effort. It is a habitual pattern of behaviour.

Yet there was a time when that signature was an affectation. Most people went through a stage when they practised a wide range of styles of signature. They experimented with pretentious loopy signatures, writing that leant forwards or backwards, circles in place of dots, etc. Only when they settled on a signature they liked, and practised it over and over, did it become 'their' signature.

We change the way we speak too, copying other people's mannerisms and trying out different styles before eventually settling on what becomes 'us' after repeated practice. We even try out opinions and attitudes before settling into who we turn out to be.

Young people express their individuality by rejecting the styles of their parents and copying other young people. Each of us is the result of a long period of experimentation and much of our behaviour, which used to be self conscious, is now habitual. We are not aware of habitual behaviour, yet almost from birth children are developing it and the older we become the more automated we become.

Children seem more inclined to learn new behaviours than older people and they tend to naturally model on their peers, rather than their parents. It is a universal trait, which is why people tend not to talk, dress and dance like their parents. When children are faced with the choice of speaking like their parents or their peers, they usually choose their peers. This becomes particularly apparent when a family moves to a new area, or even a different country. The young people pick up a new accent, even a new language, whereas their parents do not.

Young people learn new things and change their ideas frequently, whereas it is natural for older people to gradually stop following fashions and changing their views. At some stage people invariably seem to stop experimenting and carry on listening to the same sort of music, and dressing in the same way.

This is a tendency, but it is not inevitable. Some adults make a conscious decision to keep trying new experiences and learning new things. It just takes more effort to get up and do something new, and it does not come naturally.

Young people adopt the theories and opinions of people they admire. In modern culture, these may be celebrities who are encouraged to express opinions on a range of issues they know little about. The fact remains that young people seem to be innately programmed to model on their peers in preference to 'old' parents or teachers. It follows that those parents who are still hanging on to the forlorn hope that they can in some way control their children's development, might consider trying to influence the type of peer group their children are exposed to. That is the only influence they are likely to have.

Why Stop Learning?

In evolutionary terms it makes sense for older people to stop learning. Evolutionary biology teaches us that nature is economical. The Savannah didn't change much and there was a limit to how far our ancestors could travel. So, to some extent, once they had learned all there was to know about their own environment there was no need to continue using resource hungry thinking.

However, the natural tendency to fall into a rut and seek familiarity, which made evolutionary sense for our ancestors, does not equip individuals for a rapidly changing modern world. The innate tendency for older people to get set in their ways is an impediment to successful functioning. As they get older, people are naturally less likely to review their opinions in the face of new information. They are more likely to mix with like-minded people and select sources of information which reinforce their prejudices.

Market forces have driven different parts of the media to respond to these innate tendencies. They split up the market by supplying opinions and selective information which reinforce the views of their target audience, rather than challenging them with new information. In the long term this may become a threat to effective democracy.

It is possible for older people to consciously fight the innate tendency to become blinkered. Ian Gilbert (2002) recommends one strategy: he suggests that as we get older we should deliberately set out a regime of trying new experiences to 'exercise' the brain, even if it just involves reading a different newspaper, listening to a different type of music or trying a new food.

Replicating Successful Ideas

Richard Dawkins (1974) first used the term 'Memes' to describe successful ideas which spread across populations. Some are trivial, like a catchy tune or a joke. The good ones are repeated and passed on from person to person. The other ones die out. Some jokes tour the world infecting almost every culture. Other infectious ideas are more profound. From the earliest records, these infectious ideas can be traced as they developed and guided human cultures.

Ideas about democracy and political philosophy came from Ancient Greece. In the Middle East, monotheism was an idea which spread and led to the commandments of Moses, which in turn provided a rule system to govern human behaviour.

Our current ideas about morality, religion and systems of government have evolved but they are the descendants of those earlier ideas. The reason that they survive is that they continue to work. When ideas no longer work they begin to lose influence and eventually die out. This even happens to ideas which were initially successful and spread extensively. Like flu viruses, which travel the world in a matter of weeks infecting millions, they suddenly decline and become extinct if they fail to adapt to changing circumstances.

During the last century, Communism was a successful idea which rapidly took off and spread around the world. But the view of human nature upon which the system depended was incomplete and now the idea is in decline.

The flat earth society still exists, but the idea that the earth is flat, which once infected the majority of humans, is dying out.

A resilient 'meme' concerning human nature has been the idea that emotions are something distinct from rational thought. This 'meme' underpinned theories about the mind from the earliest times.

The Stoics of ancient Greece promoted the rational side of human behaviour, as opposed to the 'unreliable' emotional side. Stoicism died out as a movement, but some of the 'memes' survived. Judaism adopted some of these ideas which continued into Christian beliefs about human motivation and behaviour. Throughout recorded history a thread of common beliefs about human nature can be traced, which none of the major psychological theories of the 20th Century questioned. The basic idea is that emotions are a primitive part of human nature, which had been superseded by the development of the brain. Most people accept the idea that the rational mind in some way struggles to control the emotions.

Emotional Thinking

Recent discoveries about the brain and advances in evolutionary biology are challenging this view. We now know that the thoughts, plans and strategies which enable humans to pursue long term goals are generated by the more recently developed structures at the front of the brain. We also know that this part of the brain can suppress ideas being generated by other areas which are concerned with more immediate needs. Although the frontal lobes of the cortex are a more recent development, we are beginning to see that emotions were not left behind in the evolutionary process. The mind and brain adapted and evolved in tandem, with emotions playing a central role in cognition. It no longer makes any sense to treat thinking, emotions and behaviour separately. Emotions are an integral part of thinking and behaving. The way we feel affects the way we think and behave. The way we think and behave affects the way we feel.

The advanced structures at the front of the brain do not suppress emotions; they use emotions to suppress ideas from other parts of the brain. Emotions are used to set priorities by the most advanced structures of the brain. Emotions are an integral part of the processes which store important memories. It is the emotions which tell us what is important.

Emotions are the mechanisms by which different areas of the brain fight for control when the ideas they generate conflict. This internal mental conflict which involves the emotions produces physiological changes which can be measured.

It has been known for some time that people suffering from stress may develop health problems, such as heart disease. Now we are beginning to understand the processes involved. Internal conflicts change our mood and there is also evidence that the emotional state influences the way that people think.

Forgas (1995) reported that the more time people spend trying to think about a particular issue, the more irrelevant moods will bias their thoughts. Ciarrochi, Forgas & Mayer (2001) also show how the influence of emotions can lead to disastrous financial decisions.

Even if some of the claims about the Emotional Quotient replacing the Intelligence Quotient have been overstated, it looks as if the emotions will take centre stage in the psychology of the 21st Century.

Thinking Skills and Distortions

Just as people become limited by their habitual behaviour if they do not make a conscious effort to learn better ways, so too can they become limited by their habitual thinking. This affects their view of the world, causing them to repeat the same mistakes and misunderstandings. Some forms of habitual thinking inhibit social interactions and reduce people's opportunities to find happiness. For that reason we all have a responsibility to work on the way we think as well as the way we behave.

Stereotyping

The brain has a tendency to group things together in categories according to shared characteristics. This is called stereotyping. It is innate and is a natural part of intelligent thinking which evolved to accelerate perceptual recognition in the natural habitat.

Research has shown that people with a well formed stereotype of birds, animals, vegetables etc, can recognise members of the categories more quickly. The more examples they have seen the better they become at defining the stereotype and distinguishing examples within it.

However, humans no longer live in their natural habitat. The information overload in modern societies allows people to create stereotypes based on unreliable or incomplete information, rather than personal experience. Research shows that stereotypes learned in this way are prone to distortion and error. When distorted thinking is used to judge other people this becomes a serious problem. Often the people with the strongest stereotypes, for example about other racial groups or even asylum seekers in general, are those with the most limited personal experience of members of those groups.

People who are operating on 'automatic pilot' habitually stereotype, but those with distorted stereotypes also allow their minds to be clouded by prejudice. It is an innate tendency to which we are all susceptible. The only way to avoid this pattern of thinking is to be alert to it.

Prejudice

People sometimes take an instant dislike to somebody. One reason could be that the person reminds them of somebody else. They have subconsciously attributed the negative characteristics of another person on to this new person.

To experience an intuitive feeling about another person is not, in itself, a sign of prejudice. It might be the result of finely tuned subliminal social skills and turn out to be entirely justified - we evolved to recognise the signs of cheats. But equally it might turn out to be entirely unjustified. It is when people stubbornly refuse to review their opinions, even when they are presented with evidence to the contrary, that they are described as suffering from 'blind prejudice.'

Wishful Thinking

Another distorted form of natural thinking is wishful thinking. This can be a dangerous habit to get into, especially for policy makers. Humans tend to show a bias towards evidence which supports what they want to believe. One way to counteract this natural distortion in our thinking is to be even more diligent about checking evidence and arguments which support our prejudices than we are about those which contradict them.

Intuitive Errors

Another bug in the system is that human brains are not naturally equipped to comprehend big numbers. There was no reason for our ancestors to count more than they could carry. The brain cannot get a 'feel' for large numbers and for that reason people can make huge errors of judgement when the numbers are big. People make decisions involving millions and billions without really understanding what they are talking about.

Bill Gates, the founder of Microsoft, was talking about the memory in personal computers when he announced in 1981 that, '640K ought to be enough for anybody.' But how big was 640K? A single letter in this text takes one byte of information, and one kilobyte is 1024 bytes, so 640 kilobytes does sound big. But 1024 kilobytes adds up to just one megabyte. One gigabyte is 1 024 576 megabytes and the notebook upon which this text is being written has a hard disk capacity of 40 gigabytes, or over 40 billion bytes. The disc is already half full.

The brain you are using to read this has a trillion neural connexions, but it cannot comprehend any of these big numbers. Bill Gates is worth billions of dollars but he is not equipped to understand how rich he is.

Probability

As we know hunter gatherers did not need to deal with huge numbers. The result is that humans habitually misjudge probability, and that is important when we are involved in risk assessment. People are not equipped to make intuitive risk assessments. That is why people buy lottery tickets, fear planes more than cars, nuclear power more than coal and man made additives more than the natural carcinogens in plants. The last three examples are risk assessments which the majority of people get wrong according to the evidence.

Learning Styles

"Hear and forget, see and remember, do and understand."

Chinese Proverb

Over recent years, psychologists have become more aware of individual differences in learning style. Teachers and academics tend to be the sort of people who learn things from books and they assumed that everyone else could learn the same way. Some people do. These are the people who diligently read instructions before trying to put something together. But other people prefer practical learning. They learn by doing, through trial and error. (Sometimes they need to return to the instructions later to find out why it all went wrong.) Those who prefer to learn by listening will follow verbal instructions better than written ones. Others still like to watch somebody else and copy them.

There is no right or wrong way of learning, providing it works. The task for teachers is to try to expand their range of teaching styles to accommodate the range of learning styles.

To some extent learning styles reflect different sensory modes. People with a preference for visual learning prefer pictures and shapes. Those with an auditory preference respond best to speech, whereas kinaesthetic learners tend to have physical skills and learn by doing. Many children who find school life difficult are kinaesthetic learners. The language people habitually use can give clues about their preferred learning style. Somebody with a visual preference might say, 'Show me what to do - I can't see it - Lets look at this.'

A person with an auditory preference might say, 'Tell me what to do - That doesn't sound right - Talk me through it again.'

A kinaesthetic person might say, 'Let's do it - I've got a bad feeling about this - Take me through it.'

Most serious incidents arise because of a breakdown in communication somewhere along the way. Those with a duty of care must pay particular attention to the way they communicate as active talkers and listeners.

Information Overload

Communication is a two way process. It involves both the transmission and reception of information. Human beings transmit information about themselves all the time, but this is not necessarily communication. As warm blooded creatures, we emit infrared radiation; other creatures can see it, but other humans cannot.

We produce odours that carry a lot of information about us over large distances. Other creatures rely heavily on odours for communication, but humans less so.

We are magnetic and have our very own gravitational fields. As we go about our daily business we produce low and high frequency sound waves that can be detected by a range of other creatures. Yet even though we transmit a great deal of information about ourselves, human beings cannot detect very much of it and most of the time we are completely unaware that we are doing it.

Using the Available Information

We are also unaware of much of the information we do transmit which can be detected by other humans. As social animals we are innately programmed to signal and decode complex social information subliminally, which means we are not conscious of all the messages passing to and fro.

Other people make judgements about us, picking up information from our mannerisms, the way we dress, the postures we adopt and our facial expressions. Nobody has the option of not communicating in this way. Human beings cannot stop sending signals or prevent themselves from making judgements about other human beings. They can only choose whether to be careful or careless about it.

Human beings have a specialised innate brain mechanism which helps them to understand other human beings, infer motives from their behaviour and predict what they are likely to do next.

This subliminal social communication involves complex mental processes, although it is habitual and subconscious. The complexity only becomes evident when the system fails to function normally.

It may be a problem with this innate mental module for understanding other people which creates difficulties for those who are described as having autistic spectrum disorder.

Associations

In some of the earliest psychology experiments, dogs were taught to associate bells with food so that they would salivate at the sound of a bell. Humans sometimes make associations in a similar way with particular aspects of the environment. Some areas trigger good memories, others bad ones.

Teachers and carers can use this to their advantage by mentally linking different parts of the environment with different rule systems. For example, in one school as the children arrived one by one to a class, the teacher could welcome them from one place, and direct them to their work.

When the teacher wished to speak to the whole group, she moved to another part of the room, which was always reserved for public speaking. The pupils soon learned to pay attention as the teacher moved towards the public speaking place, without really being aware that they were doing it. Another place was reserved only for those occasions when the teacher needed to remonstrate with the group. Soon, the teacher only needed to move towards the position to get a subconscious response form the pupils.

In the psychology department at one university the students trained one of their lecturers to move towards a particular side of the room by secretly agreeing to appear keen and interested when he moved that way, and disinterested when he moved in the other direction. By the end of the session the lecturer had moved over to the designated wall and was leaning against it, none the wiser.

Of course there are ethical considerations to the notion of training people without them being aware of it. But we are already doing it. We influence other people's behaviour all the time by the way we respond to them. The choice is whether to be careful or careless about it.

In the modern world we are continually subjected to people who are deliberately using psychological techniques to manipulate our behaviour. Governments and commercial organisations have spent a great deal of money training people in presentation and sales techniques. The best defence is to understand the subconscious processes and be more aware of what is going on.

Awareness of Social Space

In social situations most people seem to subconsciously regulate their use of space. They know roughly what distance they need to maintain for their own comfort, and that of others, without really having to think about it. This is partly innate and partly learned, as the rules vary slightly from culture to culture. As a rough guide, public space can be defined as the area outside an arms reach. The distance between the elbow and finger tips is personal space, usually only used by friends and relations.

The space between nose and elbow is intimate space which is reserved for very close friends and relatives only. Entry to intimate space is normally by invitation only through subtle signals.

We only become aware of these rules when we are forced to break them. When people are artificially forced into personal space, for example in lifts or on crowded trains, they begin to feel uncomfortable. The usual response is to avoid eye contact, looking at the ceiling or floor, and avoid conversation. This increases psychological distance to compensate for the forced surroundings. As soon as people have a choice, they tend to step back into public space, where they feel more comfortable and can begin to act more naturally.

The boundary between public space and personal space happens to coincide with the point at which a swinging fist can have the maximum impact. For that reason, when carers are talking to a distressed or angry person, it makes sense to get into the habit of moving out of the danger area. Stepping back with one foot and presenting a sideways stance is not only less threatening, but also safer than facing the person square on. Football referees have become more aware of personal space after highly publicised incidents in which they were pushed and struck. Now, to reduce the risk of assault, they have been instructed to step back into public space before issuing cards to angry players.

The safe distance is out of reach. Of course this varies according to the length of the arm and the length of whatever the person might be holding at the time. In Westminster, elected members were traditionally told to 'toe the line'. This referred to a line which was drawn to allow a safe distance between opposing politicians, which took into account the length of an arm and sword.

Some people have distorted perceptions of personal space and feel uncomfortable when other people adopt normal social stances. Others tend to misread the signals and stand too close. They may not realise that this makes other people feel uncomfortable. Some children with Asperger syndrome, part of the autistic spectrum of disorders, make mistakes with these subtle social skills. With teaching and practice they too can learn the rules and develop habitual behaviours which may not come naturally at first.

Some carers habitually invade personal space without being aware that they are doing it. They might reach across one child to talk to another, or just assume a level of intimacy which does not exist. When a child complains about a carer having 'coffee breath,' the issue might actually be one of personal space.

Some people need more space when they become upset and may feel threatened when people stand too close. For that reason it is always safer to give angry people a bit more room.

Signals

All of us can unwittingly give off the wrong signals at times. Body posture communicates how people are feeling. We can sometimes detect if a person is feeling anxious, tense, relaxed or aggressive from the way they hold their body.

Unfortunately some people develop habitual ways of standing which transmit messages they do not mean to send. They might stand with one leg curled behind the other. They may ring their hands together and look towards the floor. These patterns of behaviour signal subservience, perhaps not the message a sales manager wants to give out.

Others may habitually stand with legs apart, chest out and hands on hips. This signals dominance and possibly aggression. Standing with the hands held behind the back is also a dominant posture. It also places them in a vulnerable position if another person kicks or strikes out.

When the same person keeps getting assaulted by different people they need to start looking at their own behaviour. Stance and posture are normally a good place to start. They may need feedback from a critical friend to help them become more aware of they way they are perceived and seek opportunities to practise alternatives until they become habitual.

Changing the way people behave can change the way they feel too. For example, once a person has learned to act more confidently, they report that they feel more confident, which might be a good reason for smiling, acting confident and pretending to be happy, even if you are really in a bad mood. In the long run, it might change the way you feel.

The way people act can also have a profound influence on the mood and behaviour of those around them. Group effects can be powerful and if a teacher looks glum, that mood could spread throughout the whole class. If the teacher is enthusiastic, that could be the mood which takes over for the day. Professionals have a duty to be deliberate in the way they behave. For some children, the teacher might be the only enthusiastic adult they ever meet.

When people habitually adopt postures which are perceived as aggressive they need to be aware of it, and practise other ways of standing and sitting. As a general rule the hands should be kept low and open. Some people find it more comfortable to hold their hands together loosely in front of them to stop them waving around and sending the wrong messages. This may feel unnatural at first, but after practice it can become automatic.

Some carers deliberately reduce tension in a conversation by choosing a position where their own eye level is below the eye level of the person they are talking to. Sitting down at a slight angle without a barrier, is comfortable for most people, whereas towering over another person, especially when they are sitting down feels threatening. Anybody who remembers being berated by an angry person may recall that wagging fingers, angry expressions and bulging eyes do not actually facilitate effective communication. Overwhelming body language actually drowns out the message, so sometimes children do not understand and cannot remember what an angry adult said.

Maintaining appropriate eye contact is a key social skill. We are innately tuned into patterns of eye contact. Just a few seconds of eye contact can trigger powerful feelings. Whereas too little signals a lack of interest, prolonged eye contact feels uncomfortable and challenging.

It may be natural for males to 'square up' in challenging situations and stare in a threatening manner. This is a remnant of display behaviours in which animals try to make themselves look bigger to scare off opponents. These displays may have benefited our ancestors but they are not always helpful in modern settings. Those who want to work as professional carers have to learn to behave unnaturally. With sufficient practice what felt unnatural becomes habitual.

Paying Attention to Body Language

Body language is an indicator of the sort of state a person is in. When carers first come on duty, or as people arrive, it can be useful to deliberately consider the messages their body language is giving. One successful teacher always made a point of meeting pupils at the gate first thing in the morning. If a child arrived exhibiting signs of stress, with hood pulled up, head down and hands thrust deep his pockets, the teacher would intervene before things went wrong. A ten minute diversion at the beginning of the day saved a lot of time which would have been wasted later, picking up the pieces.

Talking

Impressive displays of body language sometimes have the effect of drowning out what a person is actually saying. In addition to this people under stress do not always think or communicate clearly. For this reason it makes sense to develop scripts to use in challenging circumstances.

Maines and Robinson (1988) reported a 50% reduction in disruptive behaviours following the introduction of a more structured script for teachers to use when giving directions. Teachers were taught to use the name of the child to gain attention, maintain eye contact as they gave the instructions and use clear positive language. Then they checked understanding, by inviting the child to state what they had understood. This simple procedure could be adopted in most schools.

Faulty Scripts

Some patterns of communication which are not effective are still common. The word 'now' seems to flow naturally from angry mouths following a direction. It seldom has any effect. Another pattern of words commonly used by ineffective communicators is, 'I won't tell you again.' It tends to be said by people who are about to tell them again, usually with no more effect than the first time. Both patterns should alert us to the risk that we are becoming locked into an escalation.

Another danger sign is the use of threats. In face of defiance, the natural response is to issue a threat, and if that fails, raise the stakes by issuing an even more serious threat.

The problem with escalating threats is that they are seldom carried out and children learn to ignore people who do not keep their promises. A threat, however severe, is meaningless if it is not followed through. It is better to do something small than threaten something big. It is better still to give a clear positive instruction and allow a pause for thought. Sometimes, after a delay, children comply. Only those who are patient discover this.

The word 'You' seems to be a problem word which tumbles out of angry mouths. It can provoke conflict because it personalises the issue. Maines and Robinson (2001) suggest that communication can be improved when carers train themselves to use a script which begins with, "When you..." and ends with, "Then I ...".

For example, rather than ordering a pupil to stop tapping a pencil, a teacher might explain, 'When you tap the pencil it makes me lose my place then I cannot get on with the story.'

How to Give Attention

Effective communication follows certain core principles. Irrespective of the service setting, the aim of carers is to encourage the people they care for to communicate and interact without being continually directed or corrected. The best way to give attention is to be led by the other person. A carer might ask to join in an activity allowing the other person to lead without questioning or taking over. The carer is encouraged to enthusiastically describe what the other person is doing, rather than offer suggestions and directions. This does not come naturally, especially for those who are used to teaching. Frequent praise, along with smiles and friendly touches are also encouraged. The key is that attention should be offered freely when the person is engaged in positive behaviour, not given in response to challenging behaviours.

Praise

Particular care needs to be taken with praise. Some children with emotional difficulties do not accept praise easily, especially as most praise involves a judgement about them, or something they have done. It can be bewildering for carers when the response to a positive comment is the destruction of the very piece of work they have just praised.
A statement which relates to the feelings of the carer, rather than a judgement about the child or the work, might be easier to accept. 'I love bright colours,' rather than, 'You have painted that well.'

How to Withdraw Attention

The advice to ignore challenging behaviour sometimes produces a bewildered response from carers. It is very difficult to do, because it does not come naturally. We instinctively respond to the behaviour which captures our attention. Deliberately withdrawing attention is a refined skill, which needs a good deal of practice before it feels natural.
To start with it may be easier to focus on one 'problem' behaviour at a time. The moment a person begins to exhibit the behaviour, the carer looks away from the face, stops speaking and tries to look neutral and uninterested. They should not touch unless it is absolutely necessary. However they must keep looking for an opportunity to 'catch them' doing something positive. The key is to do nothing at all while the person exhibits the negative behaviour, but be ready to give attention immediately if they behave well.
It takes self control, observation, timing and, of course, practice.

Maintaining Communication

Keeping people interested and engaged is one way to avoid challenging behaviour. It is good practice to have a range of activities to occupy individuals, rather than expect them to wait for everybody else to be ready for a group activity. When a carer is working with a group who are engaged on an activity and notices one member losing interest, or being disruptive, it can be more effective to move quietly towards the person without interrupting the activity, rather than stopping and drawing attention to the negative behaviour.

When a carer is working with one person they can still maintain engagement with the rest of the group by intermittent scanning eye contact. This can be reinforced by positive comments acknowledging appropriate behaviour. Often, the more positive comments there are, the more cooperative people tend to become.

Powerless Scripts

There are some situations in which carers may not be in a position to enforce a direction. If a defiant child is already running away or climbing up a tree there is really very little the carer can do about it. There is no point in giving orders which cannot be enforced and carers want to avoid the 'faulty threat' scripts.

In these situations it may be more effective to take the pressure off. Telling a defiant child to stay where they are, until they feel ready to come back or climb down, may be a quicker way of resolving the problem than repeatedly issuing directions which are ignored.

Adults who flock together and stand around watching are not much help in these situations. An audience can encourage defiant behaviour, particularly if the person is trying to provoke a reaction. Carers can monitor the situation without being obvious about it. Often, behaviour is maintained by an audience, and when the audience is less obtrusive the behaviour diminishes.

Presupposition

Presupposition is a useful psychological trick. It avoids an argument by giving the impression that the parties have already moved beyond a disagreement. Asking a person to do something and thanking them immediately before they have done it, pre-supposes that they are going to comply, and in fact increases the chance that they will.

Ian Gilbert (2001) describes a teacher in a mainstream school who would take the card from a pupil on report and sign it at the beginning of the lesson, ticking the excellent behaviour box. The teacher signalled confidence and trust by presupposing that the pupil would behave well, and in that class the pupil always did.

Assertive Communication

When an interaction turns into a dispute, different scripts are required. If people become angry and the situation begins to escalate towards aggression, there is no longer any purpose in trying to pursue the original issue.

Angry and aggressive people are not rational and they do not listen, think or express themselves very well. The priority in such situations is always to avoid violence by calm defusion and de-escalation.

However, this does not mean that issues never need to be addressed. If people with challenging behaviour learn that they can evade the consequences of their actions by becoming aggressive, this becomes their habitual response. It is crucial that the original issue is picked up at a later time and followed through.

In order to be effective, assertive criticism needs to be structured carefully. The first task is to choose the right time and place to talk, so that the discussion can be completed without distraction or interruption. The carer should specify instances of unacceptable behaviour, rather than make any comments about personal characteristics. They should follow the 'When – Then – I feel' script, specify preferred alternative behaviours and state the positive consequences of coming to an agreement. The carer should allow feelings to be expressed and listen respectfully to any argument, but confirm expectations in the face of unreasonable stubbornness.

It can sometimes be helpful to choose a time for the discussion which precedes something the person normally likes, so the meeting can end on a positive note. Assertive behaviour is not aggressive but friendly and firm.

Diversions

Sometimes people find it easier to talk while they are doing something else. Helping with a job can provide a good opportunity to talk about other things. Finding, or even manufacturing, a job can be a lifesaver. It can be used as a diversion when someone is becoming angry. In one setting the caretaker was particularly skilled in helping to defuse potentially violent situations. He would ask someone who was becoming agitated to help him for a moment, allowing the person to withdraw without losing face.

A developing confrontation can often be more easily defused by one of the ancillary or office staff who is not perceived as being tainted with authority. When teams work constructively in this way they can be extremely effective, but it requires a team approach. One implication is that all members of the team should participate in training.

Help Scripts

When people are under pressure they do not always express themselves well. To avoid misunderstandings it is beneficial to develop 'Help' scripts in advance. Angry people do not process language well and are prone to misinterpret what is said. For that reason, in tense situations it is good practice to speak in short simple sentences. Carers should normally try to maintain communication at all times; however, common sense dictates that if talking is making the other person angry, the most sensible thing to do is to be quiet.

When a carer is communicating with an angry person it helps if they can act as if they are calm, confident and friendly. Using a person's name is a friendly signal, and it tunes them in to listen to what the carer is about to say next.

The basic form of the help script is three statements. The first acknowledges the problem without allocating blame or making a judgement.

'John, I can see something is wrong,' or, 'John, I can see you are upset.' We avoid the word angry.

The second message conveys that we are offering help and support. 'John, I am here to help.' Some people prefer, 'John, Let me help.'

The third message is an attempt to get the angry person to engage. 'Talk and I will listen.'

Finally the script offers the choice to withdraw; a 'get out' with dignity. 'Come along, we can sort it out.'

Angry people often pace around in these tense situations. Carers should avoid the temptation to follow them around as this can trigger feelings of a pursuit. Where possible the carer should stay still, speaking calmly, clearly and confidently.

When an angry person is making personal comments or threats, carers should be selective in their responses. They should analyse what is being said and try to respond only to the factual part, making no response to personal abuse. The only purpose of verbal attacks is to provoke a response allowing the argument to escalate. The trick is to avoid saying anything that feeds the fire in an argument.

Fight Scripts

When fighting becomes a problem in any community the strategy should be to address the fight culture, rather than repeatedly breaking up the fights. Fight cultures involve more than just the people who fight. There are often other people inciting fights, and a peripheral crowd whose presence contributes to the likelihood of violence.

As a tactic it is essential to remove either the key player's or the audience. For those who refuse to comply, there must be consequences which are followed through, so that if a similar situation arises in future they have a reason to behave differently.

If a community agrees that it does not accept fighting, it also needs to agree how individuals should signal that they do not want to become involved. People should be encouraged to acknowledge that they have a choice, and that there will be consequences for those who make the wrong choice. When a person wants to demonstrate that they are not looking for trouble they should be encouraged to turn around and walk away.

When a carer approaches a developing dispute the script is, 'Turn round and walk away.'

Team Culture

In a team culture it should become accepted that colleagues always offer help and are always willing to accept it. Aggression tends to become focussed upon whoever happens to be there. The longer a carer has been involved in an aggressive or violent incident; the more likely it is that they will be 'contaminated' by it.

This does not mean that they have done anything wrong, just that somebody new will be more effective. Carers can also become tired and upset themselves so they are not always best placed to recognise that they need a break. Sometimes changing a face enables everyone to save face. It is usually after something changes that the incident changes direction towards a resolution.

Where the expectation that help will be offered and accepted becomes part of the staff culture, it empowers all members of the team. In particular, it empowers those who might feel uncomfortable about offering help to senior colleagues. It is incumbent upon senior staff to demonstrate their commitment to this ethos by encouraging, accepting and welcoming help.

Accepting help should be regarded as a sign of professional strength. Each time help is offered and accepted, a choice-point is created which may be the diversion that helps the distressed person to begin to calm down.

Choice-points

Choice-points are like forks in a path. One route leads to aggression and violence, the others lead somewhere else. The more forks there are in the path, the more opportunities there are to defuse and de-escalate. Offering help and 'saving face by changing face' create choice-points. It is often at these junctures that a violent situation begins to calm, so the more changes carers can engineer, the more opportunities are presented to resolve the situation quickly.

Active Listening

Normally the responsibility for effective communication is shared between the sender and the receiver of information. When we act naturally we are often thinking about several things at the same time, half listening to one thing as we monitor something else. Humans are good at multi-tasking. Our brains naturally monitor information and filter out the bits which are not important. This habitual behaviour works well most of the time, but there are times when it is not good enough. Active listening is a set of skills by which the receiver takes more responsibility to ensure that communication is effective.

The job of an active listener is not only to pay attention, but also to put the speaker at ease and facilitate the information exchange. To this end, an attempt should be made to provide a relaxed, comfortable environment for the conversation. There needs to be sufficient space, privacy and time, so that talk is not rushed or inhibited.

The listener should fight the impulse to interrupt and resist the natural temptation to join in with their own story. Instead, the listener should concentrate on what the speaker is trying to say. Relevant questions may be asked to show interest and clarify points, but positive listening has to be non judgemental. The carer should give feedback to demonstrate that they are listening by:

- Facing the person
- Eye contact
- Leaning slightly forward
- Open body language
- Responding by nodding, smiling and giving verbal cues.

Active listening involves putting mental effort into thinking about what a person is trying to say and analysing the content. Listening itself is a statement of value.

Communication Differences

We should be aware that not everyone communicates in the same way. Different cultures have different rules for the margins of personal space, eye contact and the acceptable level of tactility. Signs and gestures mean different things in different countries and we all share the responsibility for avoiding offence.

When people cannot use spoken language, for whatever reason, they may be helped to communicate in other ways. Some people do not understand social interaction and cannot read facial expressions or body language. Some cannot use talking and listening, but can communicate effectively using sign language. Others may only understand a few words, objects or symbols.

Just because a person experiences difficulties in one area of communication does not mean they cannot communicate at all. It is the responsibility of those who work with children and adults with communication difficulties to help them to express their feelings and exercise choice, so far as it is practically possible.

People with poor communication skills can become isolated. Sometimes, just sharing an activity might be enough, without feeling the need to direct or teach.

But it is important to remember that a person with limited communication may have learned that the only way to influence the world is through challenging behaviour.

Behaviour is a language too.

Chapter 2 – Feeling

"Man, unlike animals, has never learned that the sole purpose of life is to enjoy it."

Samuel Butler

In order to understand our emotions we need to look at how they may have evolved. Many of our emotional responses are innate. Paul Ekman (1998) has researched human responses to facial expressions for many years. He has identified universal expressions of emotion which are shared by all cultures. These include Anger, Happiness, Sadness, Fear, Disgust and Surprise. The fact that we developed innate mental mechanisms which enable us to 'read' other people's emotions indicates that this is an important function.

Sympathy, Gratitude and Guilt are the innate feelings which drive humans to cooperate with each other by suppressing selfish, greedy habitual urges.

They evolved over time because those species which cooperated were more successful than those which did not.

However, cooperative behaviour benefits the species, rather than any particular individual. In a cooperative society it could make more sense for a selfish individual to take advantage of other people's generosity without bothering to reciprocate. A society of peaceful cooperative creatures would therefore be open to attack by cheats and bullies. As a result, systems evolved to deal with them.

Amongst these was the ability to recognise individuals, so cheats could be identified and remembered. "Once bitten twice shy" only works providing you can tell the difference between people, and remember who it was that cheated you.

Systems also developed to warn off potential bullies. This was all about bluff. Animals developed the ability to display changes in colour and behaviour which gave the impression that this animal could be mad, unpredictable and aggressive. The purpose was to persuade a potential aggressor or cheat to pick on somebody else. An ability to remember individuals was important here too. An aggressor or cheat, who believed that another animal was not only willing to defend itself, but had a long memory and would pursue him to the ends of the earth for vengeance, had good reason to choose another victim.

So there are good evolutionary reasons why our ancestors might have developed habitual responses to perceived threats consisting of dramatic displays of anger and rage.

The males in hunter-gatherer communities needed to establish a reputation for violence and retribution. This was the only protection they had. In the past these patterns of habitual behaviour must have worked for the species, but they do not equip us very well for the modern world. Many of the problems of humanity result from remnants of this innate tendency to display extreme violence and retribution.

The phrase 'going berserk' comes from the fearsome reputation cultured by the Viking Berserkers. Running 'amok' describes similar behaviours from Samoa (a society once mistakenly believed by anthropologists to be entirely peaceful.) Once again men gain a fearsome reputation for apparently uncontrolled violence. The same innate mechanisms have also driven individuals to commit dreadful massacres in modern communities. The pattern has been repeated too often for it to be coincidental.

A long standing debate in the military has centred on whether or not women are temperamentally suited to serve in front line combat. Similar questions could be asked about the abilities of men to take the backroom decisions. It can be argued that it is men, so prone to dramatic gestures, who are least equipped for modern armed services, where vast quantities of weapons can be dispatched remotely with ease. A man driven by primitive urges to settle grudges and display extreme aggression can become a risk to the whole species if he is armed with weapons of mass destruction.

There are some aggressive women, just as there are some peaceful men, but we cannot ignore the fact that men seem to have a tendency to behave aggressively.

The Development of Problem Behaviour

Babies are born with a powerful innate protection mechanism. They can make a noise which adults cannot ignore.

This is because the adults of the species are innately pre-wired to find the sound of a crying baby extremely uncomfortable. It is impossible to relax when a baby is screaming.

Young creatures of all sorts are similarly equipped to stimulate the adults of their species to give them attention and ensure that their needs are met. Later, once the innate language mechanism switches on, humans learn more sophisticated ways of getting what they want, but attention seeking is innate and it works. Children with severe learning difficulties, who do not learn to communicate their needs, may go on to develop a range of alternative behaviours which get adult attention, but cause problems for them and their carers.

Part of the normal process of experimentation for young children involves exploring and testing. This also means testing adults who try to apply rules and it begins soon after a toddler learns to toddle. Sometimes it develops into the battle of wills called the 'terrible twos.' In most families this negotiation of power is resolved. Children learn that they cannot always get their own way by having tantrums and they learn to negotiate.

But toddlers continue to work extremely hard to gain adult attention. The more attention they get the more they can learn, and toddlers are programmed to learn. Refusing a toddler attention is really not an option, because they are programmed to get it one way or another.

It is here that the seeds for some behaviour problems are sewn. The innate programme, by which children learn to get attention, has a built-in design fault. It goes wrong in the modern world when parents are not in a position to give their attention freely and spontaneously.

In extended families there was usually someone else available, but modern life does not equip all toddlers so well. There may be very good reasons why a parent is unable to give spontaneous attention. Parents may be tired after working long hours, unwell, depressed or just too busy. Unfortunately, life in modern society does not provide the support which was available in communities of hunter-gatherers where the women and children were all together.

Attention seeking is innate habitual behaviour. Even negative attention can be rewarding for young children. They cannot help it. When spontaneous attention is not forthcoming, the child provokes the parent to provide negative attention, and usually succeeds. Even if the attention comes in the form of anger, that seems to work. So long as it is attention.

Rewarding the Right Behaviour

This dangerous habitual pattern of behaviour can take hold. A toddler can become reliant on negative behaviour and begin to train a parent to express anger. A parent can unwittingly train the toddler to be provocative by rewarding the negative behaviour with attention. This maladaptive pattern is reinforced every time the parent is provoked and responds. It can be even more powerful if the response is emotional or violent. A smack, followed by guilty tears and hugs, is powerful reinforcement. The outcome of the whole performance, so far as the child is concerned, is rewarding. It is attention.

If that pattern becomes established, things can begin to go seriously wrong. Parents who are faced with a child who appears to provoke them all the time feel less inclined to offer spontaneous attention. They may respond to any brief lull in the battle with relief, but this is not the time to take a rest. This is the moment to take the initiative, by giving deliberate attention to reward any positive behaviour, because unless they get in first, the child will have to seize the initiative once again and start provoking. If parents, carers or teachers miss the opportunity to reward good behaviour the opportunities to do so become rarer.

Every time that the negative patterns of behaviour are repeated they are strengthened and the probability that they will occur increases. Some families repeat the pattern hour by hour, day by day and year by year. Soon the patterns are habitual. Children have learned that misbehaving works, and what works is repeated more and more.

The pattern can escalate into a dangerous loop of abuse with habitual provocation towards violence, followed by a rewarding emotional making up process which involves affection and sometimes material rewards.

Some children arrive at school already well versed in this maladaptive habitual pattern of behaviour. Laslett et al (1987) reported that 'some children...seek punishment, because at least it is one way of gaining attention; the punishment does nothing to alter their behaviour for the better.'

People who become locked into this pattern of interaction may grow into adults who search out abusive partners. The habitual route to affection for some is via provocation, antagonism, aggression and violence.

The idea that any attention can be rewarding, including a telling off, takes some getting used to. One way of thinking about reward is to adopt the thinking of the old behaviourists. They defined a reward as anything which increased the probability of a behaviour being repeated. So, if a child habitually misbehaves and the teacher habitually responds by shouting, then the fact that the pattern continues confirms that it is rewarding. Carers need to suppress a natural tendency to respond to such behaviour. This takes effort and feels unnatural to begin with. Telling off some children for naughtiness is rewarding. Relaxing when the child is behaving well is an understandable response, but the wrong one.

This is not to suggest that carers always have the option to ignore challenging behaviour, but even if they do intervene it may be possible to remove some of the rewarding components. Making somebody else angry is a powerful feeling which can be rewarding in itself, but it depends on carers signalling their anger. Just looking angry might be what is rewarding the behaviour. Sometimes parents and carers need to learn to control the signals they are giving.

The moment a child starts exhibiting positive behaviour is exactly the time to respond with attention. Failure to respond immediately, when the child is behaving well only encourages the child to resort back to the old negative behaviour patterns. The hardest part of the process is spotting opportunities to reward what can be fleeting glimpses of positive behaviour. It is called 'catching them being good.'

Functional Behaviour

Some children continue to exhibit problem behaviour because it works for them. They manage to be rather successful, learning to 'work the system' to get what they want. In fact, many people who go on to be extremely successful in the real world were challenging, difficult students. Opinions about what is acceptable or normal vary between families and schools, but life only becomes difficult when people cannot agree about what is acceptable. Habitual training depends on consistency.

Children like rules. In their play they often spend almost as much time arguing about the rules as they do playing the game. Once established, agreed and learned, people get into the habit of following the rules. But if rules are never clearly established, then arguments and challenges become the habitual pattern of interaction.

Patterns of challenging behaviour become habitual because they are functional. The task for carers is to identify how the behaviour is working for the individual and help to find better alternatives.

One way that challenging behaviour works in schools is that a 'bad boy' or 'class comedian' gains status. They may not impress the adults, but young people have no interest in adults. Being rude to a teacher, putting other people down and showing off are all challenging behaviours which can be enjoyable.

It has always been a natural part of growing up for children to explore power, although traditionally they did not have much power to wield. In modern western society there has been a redistribution of power, in fact empowering children has been an explicit child protection strategy. Unfortunately, not all children are able to wield power responsibly and some use it to bully others, including the adults who are trying to look after them.

Being able to trigger fear or rage in another person feels very powerful. Threatening, abusing and humiliating somebody in authority, safe in the knowledge that a professional carer will not respond, can be an extremely rewarding experience for some. It triggers some of the innate dominant / subservient display behaviours which regulate status between social animals.

Some schools and care settings encourage disturbed children to 'act out' behaviour to get it out of their system. There is no question that people feel better after having 'a good cry.' The danger comes when children are encouraged to indulge in 'therapeutic' tantrums. All the research shows that acting out anger just makes people angrier.

Habitual tantrums can be rewarding in themselves and they can also be functional in other ways. A child can learn that just threatening a tantrum gets them out of trouble. Consequently it becomes an habitual avoidance response. Children can learn that emotional displays, and other disturbing behaviours, provide a reliable escape from the pressures of work. We need to ensure that these behaviours do not become habitual. It is a mistake to assume that people are always consciously aware of what they are doing. Habitual patterns of behaviour become automatic. Rocking, head-banging or tapping can be a means of escape from boredom.

If a child vomits over his Maths book, the chances are he will get out of Maths. Nosebleeds, wetting, soiling and vomiting can all become functional habitual behaviours.

Even the physical interventions by carers can be exhilarating and rewarding, especially when adults take care to ensure that no discomfort is involved. In the animal world ritual patterns of habitual behaviour are exhibited between young males who conduct play fights to test their strength and status within the social group. Carers can unwittingly train children to seek routine restraint. They need to be aware that even bizarre behaviours can become functional if they are inadvertently rewarded.

Aggression and fighting is exhilarating, providing you do not get injured, and children seldom get injured during their fights. Some young males enjoy fighting. They go out looking for fights. Gangs of 'football supporters' organise large scale fights using their mobile phones. Aggression is clearly rewarding for many human animals.

Delinquent behaviour is the inevitable result when disturbed children learn that anti-social behaviour works for them. They need structure and support to enable them to learn better alternatives to these ultimately maladaptive habitual patterns of behaviour.

The primitive societies from which we evolved provided that structure and support. Our task is to ensure that it is not lost in our modern social environment.

Normal Responses to Challenge

A major source of stress and anxiety for most people is having their inadequacies exposed. Most people try to structure their adult lives so that they avoid being placed in positions where their weaknesses are put on public display, yet in schools and some care settings that is not always quite so easy for the clients.

Most people hate being embarrassed, and public speaking is a source of terror for many. Yet in schools children are sometimes ordered to speak in public. They find themselves embarrassed without warning in public assemblies. Often this is thoughtless behaviour by teachers, who tend to enjoy talking themselves and forget what a strain it is for others. For some adolescents, going up to shake a head teacher's hand to receive some token or prize is a torture they will happily avoid by under-achieving.

The victims of bullying are under constant pressure and may exhibit disturbed behaviour as a result. All of these in addition to the rejection, loss, and illness which are all part of ordinary life sometimes combine to create an unbearable strain. Sometimes it is a wonder that they manage as well as they do. The responses to extreme pressures are sometimes extreme. We need to be alert to the early signs of stress by learning to recognise how normal people behave when they are under pressure.

Self neglect is a typical sign that something is wrong. People under pressure may lose interest in their appearance. They may not be eating properly and begin to lose weight. They may not turn up for work or fail to cope with the work. These behaviours are mirrored by children who are under pressure.

Another typical sign is displacement behaviour. When a person is feeling bad they are often trapped with bad thoughts. As soon as they have a free moment the same bad thoughts return, like an annoying tune. A typical strategy is to do something else: anything to block out unwelcome thoughts. In the short term some children might tap a pencil or scribble on a book or a wall, make a silly noise or provoke a response by provoking somebody else.

Some people try to block it out by working ridiculous hours, doing obsessional housework, running, swimming or over exercising at the gym. Many of these are normal behaviours, taken to excess as a means of dealing with pressure. Behaviours such as rocking, crying, screaming and head-banging can be functional displacement behaviours.

Some people take refuge in over-eating, drinking, drugs and a range of binge behaviours which also offer short term comfort.

Another response to abnormal pressure is to compensate for the bad feelings by artificially trying to alter them. Some people habitually boast and tell lies to make them feel better. They repeat their stories, almost oblivious to the fact that nobody believes them. They are really talking to themselves. Boasting is not a sign of high self esteem; it is a sign of somebody desperately trying to boost low self esteem. In other publications I have used the analogy of a slow puncture to describe people with low self esteem who have to spend so much time pumping themselves up. Somebody who habitually boasts and tells lies to boost their self esteem may have a part of their personality which almost believes the lies, but at the same time have nagging doubts. Nagging doubts are the modular brain generating conflicting ideas which compete for attention. When people under pressure say they don't know what to think, they are probably speaking the truth.

Many children with emotional problems celebrate other people's failings, mocking their achievements, clothes and families, looking for ways of upsetting them. One way of building yourself up is to put other people down.

So when does it become abnormal? It is normal for people to lose weight when a relationship breaks down. At least you come out of it looking a bit better. But loss of appetite is on a continuum which can lead to anorexia and other eating disorders.

The scene in so many films in which a hero responds to some setback by getting drunk is a cliché because it is such a common response. But that is on the same continuum that ends in drink and drugs dependence.

People under pressure may pick old scabs and bite their nails. But that sort of behaviour is on the same continuum which ends in more serious self injury. The distance between picking an old scab and scratching to create a new one is a relatively small step on the continuum. Reckless behaviour is on a continuum which can lead to suicide.

Attention seeking is on the same continuum as hoax calls which can in turn lead to fire-raising. There have been tragic cases where individuals have started fires so that they could then 'discover' them and pretend to be a hero.

Many ordinary people revel in their illnesses. It is more common for people to claim that theirs was one of the worst cases the doctor had ever seen, rather than to admit it was a routine complaint. To have a number of hospital doctors rushing around trying to work out what is wrong can make a person feel important and it can become addictive. Munchausen's syndrome, when people deliberately make themselves ill, and Munchausen's by proxy, where parents cause a child to be ill, are both at the extreme end of the same continuum.

Challenging behaviour is often a response to pressure. Rather than treat people who exhibit challenging behaviour as abnormal, it is more useful to consider their behaviour as extreme examples of normal behaviour. We need to understand how they may have developed, and what needs are currently being met by them. Until people's needs are met in some other way, just telling them to stop is unlikely to have any effect.

Challenging Behaviour from Carers

Children and adults with learning disabilities sometimes find the behaviour of their carers challenging. When people are given opportunities to express their views, they complain about frustration resulting from low expectations, boring activities and dull routines. Another common complaint is that carers have favourites. Inconsistency in responses may give this impression, and inconsistency is another frequent complaint.

People in care settings are understandably sensitive about carers talking about them behind their backs or discussing their private lives and families.

A lack of sensitivity to a person's stage of development presents challenges for them too. Emotional development is not a smooth continuum. Children and young people grow at different rates, with development being typified by spurts of growth, punctuated by pauses. The educational system uses chronological age to group children, in spite of the reality that at times their emotional development varies by as much as three years.

Bigger children may not be as mature as they look and suffer unrealistic expectations from carers. Children who happen to be small resent being treated like younger children.

Adolescence is a difficult time for everyone. The long bones grow in spurts resulting in a loss of coordination and accusations of clumsiness. Hormones are out of control and at the beginning of puberty the pineal gland begins to alter sleep patterns in the brain before the body is ready for it. The result is that they cannot get to sleep at night. Even though they still need ten hours of sleep, adults shake them awake too soon and send them off to school. No wonder there are confrontations.

In order to prevent confrontations from developing into violence, carers need to develop a repertoire of habitual behaviours and scripts to avoid the emotional triggers.

The airline industry has long experience of how people respond under extreme pressure. They have discovered that people find it difficult to think clearly and creatively in a crisis, so pilots are trained to fall back on the use of scripts and checklists during an emergency. They are also trained to continually check for signs of developing problems, so that they can act earlier and respond quicker to prevent a small problem from developing into a major crisis.

Carers who may have to manage angry and aggressive people need to operate similar procedures.

Motivation & Self Esteem

The concept of self esteem is so entrenched in western culture it is easy to forget that it is a relatively recent idea. A whole industry has evolved around the concept. It is another of those successful ideas, or memes, which appeal to people and are replicated rapidly.

Self esteem is an individual's estimation of worth. For over twenty years it has been the received wisdom that one of the main tasks of child rearing and education is to build up self esteem. To this end, parents and educators have been encouraged to offer unremitting praise. Research evidence suggests we need to be a bit more sophisticated about this approach. A study published by the Joseph Rountree Foundation (2001) found that some delinquents had very high self esteem, and Bushman et al (1998) suggested that there could be risks associated with unrealistically high beliefs about self worth. Researchers identified narcissistic tendencies in some young people with very high self esteem. These young people responded with extreme hostility and aggression when their unrealistic views about themselves were challenged.

There was no evidence that low self esteem itself was associated with violence. But we do know that unrealistically pessimistic appraisals of self worth blight lives. Positive action to raise the self esteem of people whose pessimistic self image is debilitating is undoubtedly beneficial. The aim should be to enable children to have a realistic concept of their self worth, rather than confuse them by praising everything they do.

A useful definition of self esteem is the convergence of a perceived self image and the desired self image. Therefore somebody with high self esteem does not need to be successful by any objective measure. They are just happy with who they are.

Complete convergence between the ideal self and the perceived self is the state of bliss promised by some mystical religions. Mystics in this state claim to need very little food, oxygen or sleep and forego material goods. They do very little because they don't need to do anything. They already feel fine.

From a utilitarian point of view there is a limit to the number of mystics you want in your village. If everybody was entirely self-satisfied nothing would get done, for it is the gulf between perceived self and desired self which drives people to achieve.

Most people try to get a balance in their lives between work, leisure, family and friends. But balanced people may not have what it takes to get to the top. Biographies and autobiographies often paint a different picture of an individual. Autobiographies tell stories of talented people who rise to the top naturally due to their wonderful personalities. The biographies of most high achievers usually relate a different story of extreme determination, hard work, and sometimes a callous disregard for others. It is a myth that geniuses are discovered by chance and become hugely successful without really trying. It is a myth perpetuated in the autobiographies of driven achievers, who prefer that fantasy to the harsher reality that they were willing to do almost anything to get to the top. Driven achievers in sport make great sacrifices in other areas of their lives. They practise for hours every day, in all weathers, maintaining strict diets and missing out on other pleasures.

Successful business people and politicians are often extremely hard working. They proudly relate that they are in their office by half past six every morning and never home before midnight. What is it that drives a multi-millionaire to continue to work so hard, sacrificing friends and family, to make yet another million? It is the need to feel successful, to close the gap between the perceived self and the desired self.

An extreme drive to achieve can be a sign of low self esteem or other psychological problems. Many extremely successful people exhibit the same characteristics which are called problem behaviours when they are exhibited by lower status individuals. An observation was made by Robert Hare, of the University of British Columbia, that many behavioural traits which would be described as problem behaviour in lower status people are evident in the boardrooms of corporate America. He studies psychopathic behaviour for a living, and describes how psychopaths and chief executives tend to share many personality traits, in particular an ability to appear plausible and attract followers while at the same time hiding their low self-esteem.

Some occupations provide more direct opportunities to boost self esteem than others. Having people watch, applaud and tell you how good you are is an extremely effective self esteem fix. The paradox of manic depressed, miserable comedians is a familiar one. We should not be surprised to find that comedians have low self esteem. That is why they have to do it. Similarly we should not be surprised to find that so many people who choose to perform are tortured and cripplingly shy in real life. You have to be driven to do something which makes you so anxious you are physically sick, as many famous actors have admitted. What drives people is the need to boost their self esteem. Other people who seek adulation and feel the need to exercise some of the less acceptable self esteem boosters such as bullying, boasting and showing off, become politicians, barristers, hospital consultants, vicars and, yes, teachers. Before we label children, adults with learning disabilities or low status people as exhibiting problem behaviour, we should take a broader view of what passes as normal for the rest of us.

Challenging Behaviour

People have the ability to create powerful emotional responses in others without meaning to, or even realising they are doing it. Those who have a duty of care need to be honest with themselves about their own emotional responses.

Emotional responses are part of being human. We may not want to completely control our emotions, but we need to ensure that our emotions are not always controlling us. There are many situations in modern life where doing what comes naturally is not the best course of action. Some of us have particularly strong emotional reactions to particular things. We need to become aware of what they are, because these are the buttons that trigger inappropriate responses.

For example, people who work in the caring professions are confronted by situations which trigger innate disgust responses. Excrement, vomit, urine, blood and spit are all unpleasant, but caring professionals have to deal with them. Self injury, head banging, rocking, teeth grinding, masturbating, grunting, squealing and howling are all forms of behaviour exhibited by some people with learning disability.

These behaviours may not be aimed at the carers but they can be extremely wearing.

The sound of a crying baby has driven adults to violence.

The drip, drip, drip effect of persistent low level disruption, taunting and teasing is a major cause of stress for teachers.

But it is behaviour perceived as deliberate which is most likely to provoke anger.

Most adults cite bullying and pre-meditated violence towards more vulnerable children as the behaviours they find most objectionable. Yet even these are not the incidents which tend to provoke inappropriate responses from carers. What really seems to push carers buttons are defiance, expressions of contempt, sexually explicit and abusive language, threats, pushing and spitting. What really presses people's buttons is when it feels personal.

It is important to recognise that not all behaviour which is challenging for adults is a problem for the child, and not all challenging behaviour is linked to attention seeking. An autistic child may feel uncomfortable on a hot day and take his clothes off. This might be embarrassing for the adults but not for the child.

Children with Tourette's syndrome struggle to contain impulsive grunts and obscene comments. They find it difficult not to speak their thoughts, and they cannot help thinking about exactly what they are trying to avoid saying. It is not easy to resist impulsive thoughts. Try no thinking about a pig reclining in a deckchair.

Even when neurological dysfunction is part of the problem, we should look for ways to help people to manage their own behaviour. Some caring adults do children a disservice by allowing immature or inappropriate behaviours to continue into adulthood, in circumstances where the person could have learned alternative behaviours.

When high status, or popular people, exhibit challenging behaviour, it is blamed on external influences. Yet, the same behaviour from low status people is blamed on some internal defect. The reality is that there are external pressures acting on everyone. Focusing on those which can be changed is a more productive strategy than making excuses and assuming the fault lies within the person.

Fight, Flight or Giggle

It has long been known that the limbic system in the brain is involved in emotions. The limbic system is near the core of the brain and until recently was considered to be a more primitive part. It is this system that is involved in what is known as the 'fight or flight' response.

It might as well be called the fight, flight or giggle response to bring together all the related emotions. When people giggle nervously it is really a signal that the part of the brain involved in the flight or fight response is getting twitchy.

The Amygdala is the part of the limbic system which sends the message down the spinal chord to the adrenal glands, just above the kidneys. This triggers a release of adrenaline, which floods the body almost immediately making the person feel alert, increasing the rate of breathing, the heart rate, and diverting more blood to the large muscles. People can learn to recognise the feelings of arousal associated with this system as more adrenaline is released.

They may develop a dry mouth and have difficulty thinking clearly, accompanied by a detached, light headed, faint, feeling. It feels like the blood is draining away from the brain, which is exactly what is happening. As a result a person may have difficulty remembering exactly what has just happened. These debilitating effects are the reason people need well learned habitual behaviours and checklists to fall back on in stressful situations.

Displays of Aggression

"Man is the only animal that blushes. Or needs to"

Mark Twain

In fact he was wrong. Most animals display ritualised posturing performances throughout aggressive displays. These behaviours are designed to impress and are very different to the cold and efficient manner in which hunters dispatch their prey.

As human beings get angry they display a number of signs including changes in colour, expression and behaviour. These are the remnants of the old display behaviours whose function was to warn people off.

As a person becomes angry they often give warning signals. Some of these are related to physiological changes which accompany arousal. The key is to look for the changes. A person who is normally placid and becomes more agitated is fairly easy to spot. But equally telling might be a person who is normally animated, but during the course of an incident becomes atypically passive.

Significant increases or decreases in eye contact, or a breakdown in other non-verbal communication should alert us to internal changes.

If a person begins pacing, pointing or gesticulating, this too is a signal of escalating emotions. Unfocused abuse is an emergency signal which often precedes a physical attack. Other signs of arousal include:

- facial muscles tensing or twitching
- breathing becoming shallow and short

- changes in voice tone
- changes in facial colour
- wide eyes
- agitated behaviour
- repeated phrases

The Assault Cycle

Kaplan & Wheeler (1983) suggested that incidents which result in assault can usefully be divided into five stages. These are trigger, escalation, crisis, recovery and depression.

- **Trigger stage.**

Experiences trigger the emotions which begin the process, but it may not be just one incident. A person who is prone to aggressive outbursts might be sitting in a café at a table near a door which happens to have a stiff catch. A person comes in and fails to shut the door properly. The first time it happens, the person at the table may just get up and shut the door, without feeling particularly aggrieved about it.

But then another person comes in and leaves the door open. This time the person at the table gets up and slams the door, feeling annoyed. All sorts of internal changes are taking place but nobody notices.

When a third person comes in and does the same thing, the person at the table erupts, screaming, swearing and threatening violence. The immediate trigger for the aggression was the last person who left the door open, but there was no difference between the actions of the last person and the first one. What was different was the changing internal emotional state of the aggressor.

What actually triggers aggression might not be dramatic in itself, but it may be the last in a chain of events. Carers who work with people who are prone to aggressive outbursts should be looking out for signs of arousal.

A person may already have been exposed to a number of stresses and be very close to anger. Yet it is unusual, even then, for an angry person to attack straight away. There is usually an escalation phase.

- Escalation Stage

This is the gradual build up to an assault which should alert carers to what is happening. Even people who have already chosen to look for a fight seem to need the escalation phase.

In pubs, people who are looking for a fight often try to provoke somebody. They may claim that somebody nudged them or spilt a drink.

They may accuse another person of staring at them. This escalation phase involves posturing and threats, but at least it may give a warning. During this phase the priority for carers may be to try and calm the situation or, failing that, leave if they are the target for the aggression.

- Crisis Stage

The crisis stage is when violence explodes. The choice for carers is to escape or protect themselves and others, possibly using physical interventions.

- Recovery Stage

The recovery phase begins as soon as the violence ceases and may take some time. It is a mistake to believe that a person no longer presents a risk during this phase, just because they have become quiet. Body chemistry does not return to normal as soon as a person stops behaving aggressively. It can take some time to return the person to a safe condition. During this period the slightest additional stress could send them back into crisis.

The recovery phase is particularly dangerous, because during this phase people can lash out without warning.

People who have been involved in a distressing incident need support. If relationships are to be restored, time needs to be found for reflection and repair so that all parties can learn from the incident.

Training for carers should offers a range of supports, strategies and interventions for each level of a potential crisis, including the recovery and depression stages.

The emphasis, though, should be on the first two stages. In the majority of cases skilled support and intervention at an early stage can prevent the escalation towards a crisis.

- Depressive Stage

After a serious incident people may be upset for some time and need support.

- Learning Stage

What is missing from this model is the learning stage, because unfortunately it is often missing in real life. If a person is going to learn to change this damaging pattern of behaviour, something needs to happen. In care settings this is where an investment can pay dividends later. Some people need help to enable them to better manage their behaviour in the future. What is important is the sort of help that is offered.

Catharsis

The social sciences are still contaminated with outdated ideas, some emanating from the century before last. If the psychologists who advised parents not to respond to distress, in case it rewarded children for crying, are a dying breed, there are still other erroneous ideas which are more difficult to extinguish. Attractive ideas do not have to be true. Some ideas are so appealing that people are inclined to believe them in spite of all the evidence to the contrary.

At the heart of many approaches to anger management is the Freudian theory of catharsis. This idea is based on the notion that the emotions work like a hydraulic system. Ideas about 'venting anger', 'letting off steam' or 'getting it out of your system permeate our language and culture, but result from a faulty set of beliefs.

In a comprehensive review of the literature Bushman et al (1999) reported a complete absence of any experimental evidence to support the concept of catharsis.

In fact, all the evidence suggests that therapies which encourage people to 'vent' their feelings, actually makes them worse in every way that can be measured. Freud believed that expressing anger was better than bottling it up. Bushman (2002) reports that all the experimental evidence shows that encouraging people to express anger actually makes them behave more aggressively than before.

Freud is claimed as the authority for a huge range of strange therapies. Yet as researchers have re-examined Freud's own clinical record, evidence has been uncovered that Freud fabricated evidence about the clinical success upon which his reputation was based. Webster (1999) describes how he invented case histories to support his ideas and suppressed evidence which contradicted them.

An industry of therapists is still encouraging people to trawl through childhood experiences and blame their parents for their psychological problems. Psychologists used to blame parenting for autism, schizophrenia and a wealth of other ailments which we now realise are largely inherited.

Freud's ideas are attractive because they intuitively feel right. But it is often those seductive ideas that feel right which we should examine even more closely. Many psychological fads are seductive and the more we come to understand evolutionary biology and cognitive psychology, the easier it is to appreciate how we are tempted by false ideas.

Ideas about anger and aggression have been distorted by misinformation too. Bushman et al (2001) describe that, contrary to what is reported in the media, there is an overwhelming body of research evidence which demonstrates that children's behaviour is influenced by their exposure to violence and aggression in the media A wide ranging review of the literature shows the causal link between aggressive behaviour and exposure to aggression in the media to be as strong as that between smoking and lung cancer. Yet studies reported in the media do not reflect the balance of the research. Perhaps unwittingly, the media mislead the public by choosing not to publicise stories which criticise their friends. Bushman et al (2002) suggest that video games and television programmes which encourage role play may be more dangerous than films and drama.

Chapter 3 - Saying

"Stay, you imperfect speakers, tell me more"

William Shakespear

People who are prone to losing their temper may benefit from anger management techniques. Part of the problem might be the way they habitually interpret situations. Some people respond to frustrations by assuming that other people must be deliberately trying to aggravate them. When something goes wrong they habitually look for somebody else to blame and as they focus the blame on that person they find themselves becoming angry. Anger tends to be personalised.
Angry people can be helped to recognise their own physiological responses, identify the danger signs and take themselves out of the situation before they lose control.
They can also learn relaxation techniques to limit the impact of a disappointment.
Learning that people can change the way they feel by changing the way they habitually talk to themselves can be a revelation for some people. Everybody talks to themselves. Some people habitually encourage themselves and talk themselves up, whereas others criticise, and talk themselves down.
The way a person talks to themselves may be a guide to their level of self esteem. With training, people can be helped to learn new habitual scripts, which in turn can change the way they feel.
Some people spend a lot of time worrying about things they cannot change. If there is nothing they can do, there is really no point in continuing to worry about it. When a situation is getting out of hand, people need to recognise what is happening and tell themselves to back off. They need to keep reminding themselves that it is nothing personal, because most of the time it really isn't. When a person is faced with deliberate provocation it can be helpful to tell themselves that they are deliberately not responding now, but will follow it through later. Changing the words people habitually use when they talk to themselves can change the way they feel.
This is particularly true for people who find that they regularly become angry in certain situations. It can help them to find milder words to describe the situation. Finding funny words to describe scary things can also help people who are fearful. When a situation is becoming stressful

or frightening, it can sometimes be reassuring to have a checklist or a reminder of how they can take steps to change the way they feel.
Like all skills, it only begins to work if people put in the effort to practise until it becomes habitual.

Habitual Therapy

Just because we have a tendency to behave in a particular way, does not necessarily mean that we have to behave that way. We also know that people can change the way they think, feel and behave. Over a hundred years ago the pioneering psychologist William James said, 'The greatest discovery is that a human being can alter his life by altering his attributes of mind.' Changing the way we habitually think and behave changes the way we habitually feel.

If some of our instinctive behaviours are inappropriate, human beings have the capacity to suppress the habitual patterns of thinking associated with them and replace ineffective behaviours with freshly made ones. Suppressing habitual thinking and behaviour takes an effort, but over time the effort reduces until what was laboured, conscious, mental effort becomes automatic and effortless. By repeating a pattern of behaving or thinking over and over again it becomes habitual.

We can learn to behave differently, if we bother to put in the effort. Amongst the behavioural traits which are known to be strongly inherited, are tendencies to become dependent on nicotine or alcohol. But some individuals with this tendency never become dependent and others who are, choose to give up and succeed.

Human beings are capable of learning new things throughout most of their lives. Initially this takes a conscious effort, but after practice it sinks into unconsciousness. Many physical skills fall into this category. Learning to swim or ride a bike is hard work to start with, but once the skill is fixed the thinking aspect becomes effortless. It may still be physically hard work, but it takes no mental effort to remember how to do it.

The skills necessary for most sports are consciously learned, then fixed sub-consciously and automated as the result of a lot of practice. Sports people who have already automated their skills sometimes realise they are doing something wrong, but find it difficult to change. Sports coaches help them to bring those skills back into consciousness, so they can be improved. Inappropriate patterns of learned social behaviour can be replaced in the same way. Only when people become aware of what they are doing can they relearn and improve.

Many people have critical friends who are willing to make them more aware of what they need to change. Even then it cannot be done without effort and practice. For most people the main obstacle to learning is a lack of motivation.

People will claim to be highly motivated, but the part of the brain which does the talking is not always in control. When somebody decides to go on a diet, give up smoking, give up drinking or resist any short term urge, it is the mechanisms at the front of the brain doing the long term planning. But they have stiff competition from other areas of the brain which are much more interested in meeting short term needs.

The Planning Department

The part of the brain which has developed most in human beings is the 'planning department' in the pre-frontal lobes at the front of the cortex. That part of the brain has ballooned to twice the relative size compared with the brains of our ancestors. The mental effort involved in self control involves the frontal lobes. This part of the brain works hard to suppress the urges to go for immediate pleasure which are generated by other areas in the brain (let's have another drink, let's binge on chocolate or let's punch him), in favour of ideas generated by longer term considerations (let's not - because I'm driving and I could lose my licence- I'm on a diet and I want to lose weight – I'm under arrest and hitting the officer could get me into even more trouble).

This model to some extent matches subjective experience when we try to exert self control over seductive impulsive ideas. Self control is difficult. Some people find it more difficult than others, but sometimes we choose to make the effort and can resist temptation. Other times we choose not to bother.

To what extent we are capable of free will is beyond the scope of this book. What we do know is that when we experience temptation it feels like we have a choice. There is an internal battle of wills during which thinking feels like hard work. At other times ideas occur and we follow them without really noticing what we are doing.

Classic studies, conducted over half a century ago, give an interesting insight into sub-conscious thinking and behaviour. Gazzaniga and Sperry worked with patients who suffered with extreme epilepsy. For some patients, the only cure was to completely sever the corpus callosum, which joins the two hemispheres of the brain. Once this had been achieved the epilepsy was cured, but the two hemispheres could no longer communicate.

Intriguingly it was possible to communicate with each isolated hemisphere. Gazzaniga described flashing a picture of a nude woman, amidst a series of ordinary pictures, to the left or right hemisphere of a female patient. When the picture was shown to the left hemisphere, she laughed and identified the picture. When it was shown to her right hemisphere she still laughed, but the left hemisphere did not know why. When she was asked why she had laughed the left hemisphere (the one with language) replied, 'Oh, that funny machine.'

The technical term given to a brain generating false explanations for behaviour is 'confabulation'. The conscious mind believes whatever explanations the brain comes up with, but observers know they cannot be true.

Another split brain patient, called Paul, was able to allow researchers even more insight into the way the modular brains work. In most people, only the left hemisphere of the brain has a sufficiently developed language capability to allow a two way communication. But some people are different and have developed speech in both hemispheres.

Paul woke up after his operation with isolated hemispheres, both of which had the capacity for language. The right hemisphere in most people controls the left hand, and the left hemisphere the right hand. So when each hemisphere was asked a question, it could answer by writing. When Paul was asked what career he wanted to follow, his left hemisphere wrote, 'Draftsman', whereas his right hemisphere wrote, 'Racing Driver'.

The experiments were conducted at the time of the Watergate scandal in the USA. When shown a picture of Richard Nixon, one hemisphere wrote that he liked the man, but the other did not.

There were at least two people in Paul, yet he functioned perfectly well. When the 'two' Pauls were able to collude they would agree on their opinion. Neither was aware that there had ever been a disagreement. When he functioned normally the views of the left hemisphere seemed to hold sway, but the right hemisphere went along with them.

The disturbing or interesting part of this, depending on your point of view, is that sometimes we behave exactly like a split brain patient. The conscious part of our mind, the part of us we most closely identify with, sometimes adopts the role of an observer after the event. People confabulate when they try to explain why they have just carried out the post hypnotic command. Witnesses to road accidents confabulate. They come up with different accounts of what happened, often conflicting, but they believe what they are reporting to be true.

The philosopher Daniel Dennett (1991) proposed a model of consciousness called the 'multiple drafts' theory, suggesting that each time we think we redraft our memory. This model also suggests that consciousness follows behaviour rather than directing it, which is a strange thought!

Chapter 4 - Doing

"Experience is the child of Thought, and Thought is the child of action."
Benjamin Disraeli

The benefits of habitual thinking and behaviour are that they allow quicker responses when people are under pressure and free the mind to think about other things. Habitual thinking and behaviour also helps people to respond more effectively in panic situations when creative thinking often deserts them.

Habitual thinking and behaviour can involve quite complex sequences. Combinatory learning allows sections of habitual learning to be automated and threaded together to form sequences which can still be executed without too much brain effort.

We only need to think at the 'choice-points' where we link the threads together. Even a quite simple task, such as making a cup of tea, may consist of several sequences of habitual behaviour linked together. Try making a cup of tea in somebody else's house to identify the strands. There are obvious advantages in having a repertoire of automatic responses.

But if people habitually react to a particular situation with the wrong response, that is not so good. The downside of habitual behaviour is, as football crowds chant at referees, 'You don't know what you're doing.' Drivers who daydream for miles sometimes miss their turning, end up in the wrong place, set off speed cameras or fall asleep at the wheel. Learner drivers never nod off.

Controlled Aggression

The concept of 'losing your temper' is one which is generally accepted, and it is quite common to hear people threaten that they 'won't be responsible' for their actions. Some even boast that they regularly 'lose it'. But when one part of the brain 'loses it' that just means another part has taken over. It is the frontal lobes, which are linked to consciousness that report 'losing it.' We have not access to the mechanisms which take over as they are subconscious.

Which habitual patterns of thinking and behaviour take over when the frontal lobes 'lose it' depends on two factors.

1. The repertoire of innate habitual programmes available

2. The extent to which these have been replaced by learned habitual programmes which have become automated after repeated practice.

People are not really out of control. They are just under a different form of control. One demonstration of this is the way innate habitual mechanisms seem to prevent violent males from destroying their own genes. Genes which programmed people living in social groups to destroy their own genes would be unlikely to survive, so a safety mechanism is built in.

One of the drawbacks of living in communities as social animals is that the people nearest to you tend to be relatives – the carriers of the same genes. Genes programme people to protect those genes.

It is often quoted as an established fact that people are more likely to be murdered by a relative than a stranger, but this turns out to be untrue. In biological terms, relatives are those who carry the same genes. We call them blood relatives. A quarter of murders are committed by what are loosely called 'relatives' in modern societies, but only a minute proportion of those are blood relatives.

This explains how we have survived, but it also suggests something else. Aggression cannot be indiscriminate because people evidently control it to prevent them killing the carriers of their genes. So, even those who claim to be out of control are not entirely out of control after all.

Very few people lose their tempers indiscriminately. They are much more likely to 'lose their temper' with people who have less status and power. They tend to 'lose their temper' with people they do not fear. The habitual behaviours associated with 'losing your temper' are different from those associated with feeling angry and acting assertively.

They are often ritualised. Habitually aggressive people are often bullies who have learned that this pattern of behaviour works.

People can make themselves angry by behaving aggressively, but they do not have to be angry in order to behave aggressively. Bullies only get angry with their victims when they cannot get their own way. Violent robbers have nothing personal against their victims. Barristers are not really angry with the people they intimidate, berate and reduce to tears. Children learn that tantrums work for them. In common with much of our habitual behaviour, people may not be aware of what they are doing, or why they are doing it. But that does not mean that they are out of control, any more than a day dreaming driver is out of control. It also means that they can learn to behave differently.

Self Control and Habitual Therapy

In the 1960s Walter Mischel, a psychologist at Stanford University, left a group of four year old children in a room with a plate of marshmallows. He promised that if they did not eat a marshmallow, he would give them two when he came back. He kept them waiting fifteen minutes, which is a long time for a four year old.

Not surprisingly some could not resist the temptation to eat a marshmallow.

Ten years later the group was followed up as adolescents with striking results. The four year olds who were unable to resist the temptation were easily identifiable as adolescents. The ability to resist the marshmallow test turned out to be the most reliable predictor of academic results in the standard assessment tests at 14 years old, twice as powerful as IQ tests. The impulsive children at four were still showing no sign of learning self control at 14 years old. They were also typified as having poor social contact; they were stubborn, indecisive, easily upset by frustrations, likely to think of themselves as bad, immobilized by stress, mistrustful, jealous and liable to overact to irritation with temper. In other words they all showed signs of emotional and behavioural disturbance.

They were also still unable to resist temptation and were more likely to be involved in smoking, drinking and drugs.

We now know that self control involves the frontal lobes of the brain suppressing the impulsive ideas generated elsewhere. The frontal lobes of the four year old marshmallow eaters were unable to suppress the impulsive ideas. This could be due to some innate weakness, but there is an alternative explanation.

Perhaps the children who were able to resist the marshmallows had developed habitual responses which made it easier to resist temptation. Perhaps through training and repeated practice they had developed more effective habitual behaviour.

People who are fortunate enough to be equipped with protective patterns of habitual thinking, feeling and behaving do not seem to suffer the mental effort associated with genuine self control.

As adults they may underestimate the benefits of their own habitual training and become sanctimonious about self control, claiming the moral high ground by convincing themselves that they are somehow stronger than other people.

But 'self control' is only required when a person has to make an effort to suppress habitual thinking and behaviour.

It takes no self control for a non-smoker to refuse a cigarette. It takes no effort for a person who is not addicted to heroin to get through the day without it. It takes no effort for a person who is not a habitual shop lifter to get around the supermarket without stealing something. The impulsive idea to steal never occurs to them.

True self control is when the 'planning department' in the frontal lobes is working hard to suppress impulsive short-term focused ideas. Alcohol inhibits the activity of the planning department, resulting in people getting into trouble at office parties and weddings. Most people find it very difficult to resist short term temptation, which is why so many of us smoke, drink, over-eat and do things we regret. It is habitual training that protects us.

Avoidance – De-escalation - Defusion

Past behaviour is the best guide to future behaviour, so good records of past behaviour are invaluable. Plans should share information about what has been tried, what has been found to work and what does not work. There should also be warnings about specific risks. A positive planning strategy is to consider what is different about the times when things go well and try to build on those features. Children, adults with learning disability and their families should be as involved as possible in the formulation of any plans which affect them.

We cannot do anything to prevent bad weather happening, but we can prepare for it. Similarly, some environmental influences on behaviour may be outside our control but the effects can be anticipated. Analysis of the records may indicate that behaviour difficulties tend to arise at particular times of the day, week or year. The weather itself can cause problems. Some people are upset by thunder or the sound of strong winds. Bad weather may prevent people from getting exercise. Wet playtimes are a notorious problem for schools.

Christmas or 'Red Nose Day' can be bewildering times for people with autistic spectrum disorder who need predictable routines. Carers may not be able to entirely prevent these pressures but they can take some steps to ameliorate the effects. In an inclusive setting which caters for a broad range of needs it would not be reasonable for people to miss out on the fun, but perhaps part of the environment could be kept the same as a sanctuary for those who find all the changes stressful.

Changing a proposed activity to another time, ensuring a higher staffing ratio or involving somebody who has a good relationship with a vulnerable person could reduce the risk.

When it can be anticipated that there might be problems during a particular activity, it makes sense to have a fall back plan, rather than plough on regardless with something that is not working.

This is all about risk assessment and awareness. Carers with a responsibility for people who have the potential to exhibit challenging behaviour should consciously check the emotional barometer at regular intervals looking out for who is excited, who is oppositional, who is withdrawn and who is getting bored.

The ability of carers to respond effectively to the needs of the people they care for depends on a considered and proactive approach. The experiences which affect feelings and drive behaviour are not just events. The background environment effects the way they feel and behave. Some environments feel comfortable and safe; others contain irritating features. Some schools have piercing buzzers or bells which go off at regular intervals throughout the day to signal lesson change. Some care settings have panic alarms which actually create panic when they are set off.

Relaxing Surroundings

Social scientists in the middle of the last century wanted to believe that all human behaviour could be explained in terms of learned culture. They dogmatically refused to believe in innate human behaviour. Social engineering was based on the belief that human behaviour and culture was all learned. Social scientists believed they could manipulate culture to improve human behaviour. They also believed that people would learn to appreciate their visions for a modern society. The great social engineering experiments conducted in Cambodia, China and the Eastern Block failed because modern human beings are still driven by primitive needs. Human cultures evolved to reflect the innate needs of human beings. Those imposed by social scientists, who hoped to change human nature, would always feel alien.

Evolutionary psychologists try to understand our natural preferences by looking at how they evolved to protect our ancestors in the past. The environments in which modern human beings feel most comfortable tend to share features of the landscapes in which their ancestors evolved. Humans naturally try to recreate echoes of these natural environments in their artificial habitats.

The sort of art which gives clues to our natural preferences is the mass produced variety: posters, prints, paintings and screensavers, rather than the exhibits which populate fashionable galleries. Wallpapers, fabrics, household ornaments and garden features reflect innate preferences which are present in all human cultures.

People seem to be drawn towards images of landscapes and environments which contain memorable features that make them easy to explore. They are not so keen on images of environments which are completely exposed, or those which are completely enclosed.

People like images of trees and water. In fact they like to be near trees and water, enjoying changes in elevation and places of refuge with multiple paths leading in and out. Gardens are often designed in accordance with these natural preferences. People create ponds with artificial running water. Humans like to surround themselves with images of animals and plants. Flowers and leaves are the single most common human design, because humans are innately drawn to them. They helped our ancestors to learn and remember which plants provided food and which were poisonous.

Humans are drawn to pictures of sunrises, sunsets and storms, which provided valuable warnings of changes in the weather. All these clues about the sort of environment in which human beings feel comfortable should help us when we are planning environments for people who need to feel secure.

Ecological strategies involve making an assessment of the environment in which people live, with a view to reducing the stresses and triggers which contribute to the genesis of anxiety and challenging behaviour. Another form of ecological strategy involves conducting a survey of the environment to identify objects which may be used as weapons, areas which are difficult to supervise, entrances and exists which pose problems, and features prone to damage and abuse.

A risk assessment and risk reduction approach looks at ways of removing or reducing those aspects of the environment which are uncomfortable, preventing access to dangerous areas and items, improving the use of space and replacing unsafe furniture and fittings with safer designs which are more comfortable and less prone to damage and misuse. However, the environment is not just about physical features. People need entertainment, clean air, warmth, food and drinks. When people do not take in sufficient liquids they become dehydrated, and this can affect the way they behave. The brain is largely made up of water and is especially affected by dehydration. Yet some settings do not provide easy access to water. Some schools do not provide drinking water or even allow drinking during the school day.

Some settings provide such a poor level of sanitation that people are reluctant to use the toilets. A survey conducted by Newcastle and Gothenburg Universities in 2003, reported that half the children questioned never used a toilet at school. This means that many young people experience discomfort throughout the school day.

In modern family life many children do not eat breakfast. We know that some people suffer from low blood sugar, and that it makes them irritable and bad tempered. Breakfast clubs are a successful feature in some schools.

Experiments conducted in the 1950s and 1960s on laboratory rats showed that environmental pressures increased aggression. Depriving laboratory rats of sleep, food, water and space makes them extremely ratty. Yet we pile similar stresses on human beings and are surprised at the results.

The task for carers is to assess those features of the environment which may be contributing to the feelings which drive challenging behaviour. Ensuring that the toilets are clean and operational, that drinking water is readily available and that people with low blood sugar are offered a snack in the morning are simple ways of reducing stress.

Some people become agitated if they are too hot or too cold. Some forms of lighting affect people. Some people struggle to cope in large groups, others in small ones. Good recording systems may alert carers to the particular environments which trigger problem behaviours in individuals. However there are simple changes which could be made to the environment in most settings which could significantly improve the quality of life and reduce the pressures which contribute to challenging behaviour.

There are also often simple modifications which could be made to the environment to reduce the risk of injury when people do exhibit challenging behaviour.

In schools, if there are angry children who sometimes storm out, or have to be physically withdrawn, it makes no sense to position them a long way away from the door and then put obstacles in the way.

Those who pick up everyday items and throw them or use them as weapons are much more likely to do so in an environment where such objects are easily available. The reason teachers used to throw chalk and board rubbers was that they were the weapons to hand. Angry people see everyday objects as weapons. When items are not being used they should be put away, which means there should be somewhere to put them. Untidy environments are dangerous environments. Lack of storage is a common feature of many care settings.

Gardens and playing fields seem to accumulate sticks, stones and a variety of other potential weapons. It can be helpful to hire a skip on a regular basis and completely clear the site of potential weapons.

Good recording systems might highlight the fact that behaviour problems tend to happen in particular places. There may be features of the environment which are contributing to this. In one setting a long narrow corridor led to a single door which opened inwards. Many incidents seemed to happen in that corridor. Just changing the direction of the door improved the situation.

People in glass houses should not throw stones, but equally people who throw stones should not be accommodated in glass houses. It is an embarrassing fact that some of the worst examples of accommodation for people who present challenging behaviour have been purpose built.

In any environment in which people sometimes kick out in anger, consideration should be given to removing any glass below waist height. Doors in particular should not have glass panels at the bottom.

Flat roofs are always a problem and easy access presents a health and safety risk, as do trees which are easy to climb. It is sometimes possible to reduce the ease of access to these dangerous areas. The lower branches of trees can be trimmed to make them less easy to climb.

According to all the guidance it is preferable to sit down with a person who is being held to prevent dangerous behaviour, rather than risk being taken to the floor. In environments in which these circumstances can be anticipated, consideration should be given to the strategic placement of suitable seating in key areas. The choice of suitable chairs can provide a safe and comfortable place to sit with a distressed person and also provide an additional amenity. It might be possible to line the walls behind the seating with a soft material such as cork board, to reduce the risk of banging heads. Where risk can be anticipated carers have a responsibility to take action to reduce it.

Mirrors can brighten up a dark or cramped area, and if they are flush mounted onto a prepared surface they can be made safe. People seem to like looking at themselves. In one New York office block the management was considering an expensive refit to replace all the lifts, following complaints that they were too slow. Instead, somebody creative suggested installing full length mirrors next to the lift door on each floor. The complaints stopped, because people no longer noticed the wait. Time flies when you are looking at something interesting.

Strategically placed mirrors can also help with supervision by opening up hidden corners where bullying sometimes takes place.

Environments which are clean and bright have a positive effect on people's moods. The harsh lighting in some care settings contrasts with the soft lighting people choose for their own homes.

There are probably many aspects of our own work environment to which we have become habituated, so we are no longer really aware of them. When people are house hunting they visit other people's houses and immediately spot all sorts of minor faults. It can be tempting to wonder why the householder did not do something about them before trying to sell the house. The reason is that the householder became habituated to the faults and ceased to notice their existence. We all tend to habituate to our own environments. Try putting your watch in your pocket without looking at it and drawing a sketch of all the features you can remember. You will find that you no longer notice many of the features, and have probably completely forgotten many of them, even though you look at your watch several times everyday.

It can help to ask an outsider to come in and look at the work environment through a fresh pair of eyes. They may see things that we miss, and make useful suggestions to help us make improvements. The favour can be reciprocated.

Routines

Most people feel more comfortable in surroundings with a familiar structure. Children identified as having special educational needs particularly benefit from routines and rituals.

Over the past few years a growing number of children with emotional and behavioural difficulties, attention deficit / hyperactivity disorder, moderate learning difficulties and mild autistic spectrum disorder have been included in mainstream educational settings. These children also benefit from familiar routines. In fact the need for consistency and familiar routines is a feature of almost every special educational need. Perhaps we should build in more routine to all care environments. Routines help to make life predictable and some people react badly when they are changed without warning. If there is a need for a change in routine, care should be taken to explain what it going to happen and why.

Rituals and routines evolved over a period of many years in traditional schools. Many primary children, who may have missed the religious significance of school assemblies, nonetheless found comfort in the routine chanting of the Lords Prayer, after a hymn and a story. Assembly gave excited children time to calm down and compose themselves before classes began.

Children would habitually line up at the end of playtime, or respond to a whistle by standing still. 'Hands on head' or 'arms folded' routines helped children who would otherwise be fiddling or annoying somebody else.

Children who habitually put up a hand to answer a question never had to think about it and avoided constant nagging from the teacher. In many ways rituals and routines make life easier for everyone.

Some schools abandoned many of the traditional routines in the mistaken belief that they were giving children more freedom. They failed to recognise that, in doing so, they took away the structure upon which many children depended.

Some orderly primary classrooms had rituals for organising equipment, with a place for everything and everything in its place. Routines about tidiness, picking up litter, in-seat behaviour and putting chairs on tables, all helped to reduce the number of directions necessary, and it is often interactions involving directions which provoke challenging behaviour. It can help children with behaviour problems if rituals and routines can be established and practised for the situations where problems often arise, such the first and last five minutes of lessons, entering and leaving classrooms etc. These habitual behaviours make life much easier. People need structure to help them to control their own behaviour. Initially rules can be discussed and negotiated, but once agreed they need to be taught and practised. They also need to be enforced if rules are to be maintained, which means breaches must be followed through without exception.

Issues Surrounding Training in Positive Handling

People who display difficult and sometimes dangerous behaviours face carers and policy makers with major challenges. Reports of abuse in care systems have resulted in understandable panic responses in which staff have been suspended or dismissed for inappropriate conduct. But blaming individuals is the wrong response. The only way to prevent abuse is to improve the systems which allow individuals to fail. Carers, and the people they care for, deserve to be protected by unambiguous policies, clear guidance and effective training.

In the past policy makers abrogated their responsibilities by ignoring the problem of challenging behaviour. Fearful of promoting the wrong sort of training, they failed to provide any training at all. Simplistic policies instructed carers to avoid physical intervention at all costs, with disastrous results. Intended to protect the management, they failed to protect carers or the people they were supposed to be looking after. Professional carers need to know what they are expected to do. They need to be able to use de-escalation skills and to know what they should do if those skills alone fail to bring the situation under control.

They have the right to be equipped with safe and effective strategies and techniques to enable them to intervene when someone presents a danger to themselves or others.

Under Human Rights legislation children in schools and people who are being cared for in other settings have the right to enjoy their possessions, be kept safe from harm and free from fear. They also have the right to expect that carers will take effective action to protect them from others who may damage their property or place them at risk of harm.

Risk can never be eliminated, but where it can be anticipated there is an obligation on those with a duty of care to conduct an assessment and make some attempt to reduce it. We need to be honest and open if the reality is that staff are becoming involved in physical interventions of any kind.

Restrictive physical intervention is an uncomfortable subject and people try to avoid uncomfortable subjects. One way to avoid it is to stay as far away from people who exhibit dangerous behaviour as possible. Some policy makers avoid experiencing the issues at first hand by retreating into academia and becoming experts without expertise. Even some of those who still work in dangerous settings manage to protect themselves by ensuring that somebody else is in the firing line. There are still care settings where the front line staff exhibit scars from bites and kicks, while managers with unblemished skin deny the need for training in safe and effective disengagement techniques.

Academics who have never tried out their ideas in the real world produce erudite policy principles and then make judgements on the failures of carers to translate them into practice.

Uncomfortable as it may be, it is the responsibility of policy makers and managers to give clear guidance. Anybody who claims expertise and chooses to offer guidance should be prepared to give unequivocal answers to clear questions such as, 'what do you expect us to do if that does not work?'

Clarity of Language – Clarity of Thought

It is crucially important that we are open and honest about this sensitive issue. There are still instances of policy makers protecting themselves from having to face unpalatable truths by playing with words and talking in euphemisms. The danger is that they begin to believe that the real world is as safe as the bland language they use to describe it.

When military experts talk about ordinance or collateral damage, they are deliberately using bland words to disguise uncomfortable ideas.

Collateral damage feels very much like being blown to bits when it happens to you.

In the social sciences linguistic politics sometimes seem to take precedence over clarity of expression when policy makers are faced with the uncomfortable reality that human beings attack and injure people who are trying to care for them.

The writings of social scientists can be turgid, convoluted and impenetrable as they bathe in euphemisms to avoid the truth, but the danger is that insipid language can disguise woolly thinking. Unless people are encouraged to think through all the issues, and communicate them clearly, then policies and guidance become vague and confused. In the absence of clear guidance it tends to be the carers who are left exposed. We must not allow people who influence policy to evade unpalatable truths. Euphemisms have a limited shelf life, because they only work for as long it takes for everybody to realise what they mean. Then, new words have to be found to prolong the deceit. Restrictive Physical Intervention used to be called Physical Restraint. By the time you read this, it might be called something else, because physical intervention is not something people want to think about.

In the joint guidance issued by the Department of Health and Department of Education and Skills (2002) the term 'Restrictive Physical Intervention' is used to describe any situation involving the use of force to control a person's behaviour. Although it appears to have been drafted for adults with severe learning disabilities the guidance actually applies to any school, health or care setting in which physical restraint has been used, or in which staff have ever had to separate a fight or move a child. Physical interventions are defined in the guidance as:

> 'A method of responding to the challenging behaviour of people with learning disability and/or autism which involves some degree of direct physical force which limits or restricts the movement or mobility of the person concerned.'

However it is a mistake to limit consideration of challenging behaviour to the relatively small number of people who are labelled with some form of learning disability or personality disorder. Challenging behaviour, aggression and violence are mainstream issues. People in some care settings may find the behaviour of their carers to be extremely challenging. Most of us exhibit challenging behaviour at some time during our lives, and it comes in many forms. People in positions of power may not need to resort to violence to get what they want, but they can be aggressive and domineering in other ways. The pen can be mightier than the sword if you are literate and witty, so academics attack each other in print. Those denied such opportunities, for whatever reason, use whatever means they have at their disposal. For some, the habitual response is aggression and violence.

Aggression and violence are not rare aberrations. The evidence suggests that they are a fundamental part of human nature, even though several leading social scientists of the last century pretended otherwise. Human beings have demonstrated the capacity for selfishness, aggression and violence throughout recorded history, in every race and culture studied. Early anthropologists, such as Margaret Meade, claimed to have discovered free loving, peaceful cultures hidden in the jungles of Samoa and proclaimed this as evidence that man was naturally peaceful. These notions were later exposed as false. The anthropologists turned out to be more naïve than the tribes they were studying, who did not tell them about the rape, murder and cannibalism they practised (Pinker 2002). In the bell shaped curve of a normal statistical population, people who are especially aggressive and violent will represent a small group at one end of the curve, with a similar minority who are abnormally peaceful at the other. Most of the population occupy the normal range towards the centre, but even within the normal population, aggression and violence are not entirely absent. Social scientists may not be representative of the general population. Most normal children exhibit temper tantrums at some time or other, and so do some adults. They do not consider themselves to have special educational needs or a learning disability. They blame other people for making them angry.

Of the 20% of children in mainstream schools who are identified as having special education needs at any one time, a significant number are described as having social, emotional and behavioural difficulties (SEBD). The term 'special educational needs' can be misleading when applied to this client group because many of these children do not have learning difficulties at all. Some are street wise youngsters who are considerably more knowledgeable than their teachers on a range of issues. They just cannot cope with school regimes.

Others have emotional problems but not necessarily learning difficulties. Some people with emotional problems are extremely talented - even gifted. Many who have attended special schools for young people with emotional and behavioural difficulties have gone on to be extremely successful. Nonetheless at times these children exhibit extremely challenging behaviour which is different in nature from the non-deliberate behaviours exhibited by people with severe learning disabilities and autism.

We need to be careful that we do not carelessly slip into stereotyping and prejudice when using the label 'challenging behaviour.' It is not helpful to label people in such a way that encourages unwarranted assumptions about their mental capacity or implies differences which may not exist in reality. Ordinary human beings respond to extraordinary circumstances by displaying challenging behaviour, and even the most extreme challenging behaviours share many similarities with those exhibited by ordinary people on a day to day basis.

There are genuine differences between individuals, just as there are many similarities between groups of people with severe learning difficulties, autism and other neurological disorders. However, challenging behaviour and physical interventions do not only relate to people with severe learning disabilities. The challenging behaviours exhibited in the prison service, mental health settings and schools are very different and require different approaches.

We must be careful not to allow policies and practices developed for a small unrepresentative group to be generalised into all other settings. It was the repeated failures to appreciate differences in context which contributed to significant policy errors during the latter part of the twentieth century.

The Development of Training and Guidance

In the 1980s, in the prison service, officers were being assaulted and injured on a regular basis because they were not trained in safe and effective methods of controlling and restraining violent prisoners. It was only after Aidan Healey and his colleagues led the way in developing techniques of Control and Restraint (C&R) that injuries to officers and inmates were significantly reduced.

The effects of training were dramatic. Brookes (1988) reported that sick leave, as a result of assault, fell by 82% at HMP Gartree in the year after C&R training was introduced. No inmates who had been recipients of C&R techniques had received injuries requiring medical treatment.

It is reasonable to ask why it took policy makers so long to acknowledge the reality of a problem which had clearly been evident for centuries. Those who impeded the development of training in these high risk settings shared many of the same motivations as those who blocked training in health care settings and schools. They didn't want to believe it was necessary.

The government was delighted with the results and there were immediate pressures to introduce the techniques into secure mental hospitals, and they later spread throughout the Health Service. However there were problems with taking a programme developed for one particular service setting and introducing it uncritically into a different setting. Aidan Healey expressed regret that the differences in context were not given sufficient consideration at the time. The form of C&R which had been introduced into the prison service was developed specifically for that context by a team with personal experience of working in those settings.

Differences in context are crucially important and the failure to appreciate this continued to blight government policy throughout the 1990s and beyond.

Just as the techniques developed for intentional violence and aggression may need adapting for settings serving people with severe learning difficulties, techniques developed for adults with severe learning disabilities are not appropriate or effective in other settings.

The stated aim of the BILD Code of Practice (2002) was to 'establish consistency of training' across all services, including adults with a learning disability and/or autism and pupils with special educational needs. However, consistency of training within similar services should not be confused with uniformity across all service settings. Young people with emotional and behavioural difficulties present very different challenges compared with adults and children with severe learning disability and autism. McDonnell et al (1991) warned against introducing techniques into settings for learning disabilities which had been developed to control groups presenting entirely different needs and challenges.

A common problem was that many of the people who were invited to make policy on the management of unsafe behaviour had no relevant personal expertise or experience. Edwards (1999) suggested that too often the debate reflected the strongly held views of academics, rather than those of staff who actually had to face violence as part of their work. Where training has been successful, it has usually been developed by people with personal experience and expertise within the relevant setting. It is a mistake to assume that programmes developed for adult services are necessarily appropriate for children.

De-escalation strategies designed for people with severe learning difficulties exhibiting uncontrolled behaviour may not be appropriate for people of normal intelligence exhibiting deliberate behaviour.

Some physical techniques developed for adult males do not work with flexible females and children.

Techniques developed for small children can be dangerous if attempts are made to use them on larger children or adults.

David Allen (2001) was still expressing concern at a 'bewildering array' of different training types represented by training providers registered in the BILD database. He was looking for the 'optimum training model' for all carers of children and adults with learning disability, autism and special educational needs. It is a mistake to assume there can be an 'optimum training model' for all contexts.

Like the prison service in the early 1980s, staff in secure children's centres in the 1990s received no training in the control of dangerous behaviour. Some policy makers, without the benefit of personal experience, questioned the need for physical interventions in children's settings. But children and young people can present significant risks: to themselves and others. So can untrained staff.

On the day the Department of Health (DoH) launched its guidance for children's homes, 'Permissible Forms of Control', in 1993, two film crews from rival channels were waiting outside the conference hall trying to find people who were willing to be interviewed about physical restraint. They were chasing a story about the children's centre at Aycliffe, in County Durham, whose director was speaking inside the hall.

Carers at Aycliffe had been trained by prison officers in techniques which had not been specifically designed for children. Over a period of eighteen months three young people had received fractures. Once again the mistake resulted from a failure to appreciate the importance of context.

At that time the available training came from three main sources. There were personal safety courses, delivered by martial arts experts, some of which involved 'bash and dash' strategies. These techniques involved hurting the attacker to enable escape.

Then there were techniques developed in the USA for adults with severe learning difficulties.

Finally there were the C&R techniques from the prison service, which had been introduced into health settings and were beginning to be adapted.

There was no training designed specifically for children.

In recent years the term 'Control and Restraint' has been used carelessly to describe a huge range of different techniques. Strictly speaking it should only be used to describe the original prison service techniques. In the early 1990s The National Control and Restraint (General Services) Association (NCRGSA) was set up by Aidan Healey to develop more specialised training for different service settings.

Paterson & McCormish (1998) reported significant changes in emphasis in the training being offered in hospitals under the C&R banner towards the end of the 1990s. In all areas trainers were moving away from a coercive ethos towards a shared value base centring on improved communication, de-escalation and pain-free restraint where possible.

In 1997 George Matthews developed Team-Teach, a training programme specifically designed for use with children, which went on to be used extensively throughout the education system.

In 1994 the British Institute of Learning Disabilities (BILD) and the National Autistic Society (NAS) had obtained funding to develop policy guidance around the use of physical restraint. Their study was limited to the forms of violent or aggressive behaviour exhibited by people with severe learning disability and/or autism.

The result of this work was a publication called 'Physical Interventions: A Policy Framework' (1996). This provided good context specific guidance, illustrated with a number of scenarios describing good and poor practice in the field of learning disability and autism.

There was a clear need for similar context specific guidance for other service settings. In particular, there was a request from schools catering for children and young people with severe emotional and behavioural difficulties. They wanted guidance and training which was relevant to their particular area of expertise. Without it, there was always the risk that the BILD guidance would be applied in contexts which had not been considered by the authors. In fact that was exactly what happened.

The reason was that the government's priority was to issue guidance for mainstream schools. Government policy in the late 1990s was the inclusion of more children with behaviour difficulties into mainstream settings. Professional associations were complaining that more of their members were being assaulted or injured trying to separate fights in mainstream secondary schools. Primary schools reported growing numbers of children exhibiting severe temper tantrums and aggression towards other children. Even in nursery schools, carers were receiving back injuries during attempts to lift or hold struggling young children. As soon as they were reported, these became foreseeable risks under Health & Safety legislation. It was no longer possible to pretend that there was no need for guidance and training in safe and effective physical interventions.

Yet many carers still felt uncertain about what they were supposed to do in these situations. Some staff found themselves facing disciplinary actions after being informed that their actions were inappropriate, yet the opinions about what was appropriate seemed to vary widely across the country.

Throughout the 1990s carers had been getting mixed messages, and the inconsistencies in the advice they were getting reflected genuine differences of opinion at both local and national level. What was unjust was that people's careers were being sacrificed as the experts debated.

Social Services Departments looked towards the Department of Health for advice and guidance whereas schools looked towards the Department for Education and Employment (which changed its name to the Department for Education and Science, then the Department for Education and Skills).

Confusion was particularly acute in residential schools. Schools provided almost as many beds as Social Services children's homes, but the cultures in schools and children's homes were often different.

Schools had a tradition of discipline, which did not fit comfortably with some Social Service Departments.

Some children's homes adopted approaches to discipline which did not fit comfortably with the approach in schools.

Differences of opinion were not confined to those between the departments. There were debates within the departments too. To complicate matters further, the Chief Inspector of the Social Services Inspectorate didn't agree with the way some Social Services Departments were interpreting the DoH guidance. Sir Herbert Laming wrote to all Directors of Social Services in 1997. He instructed them to inform carers in children's homes that they were expected to physically intervene to prevent children from coming to harm.

This came as a surprise to many, who had been told that the Department of Health's own guidance forbade it.

In 1998 the Department for Education and Employment issued Circular 10/98, the first guidance on reasonable use of force in mainstream schools. The letter which accompanied Circular 10/98 promised that additional guidance for specialist settings would follow.

The department had invited researchers from the University of Birmingham to identify good practice in schools for children with severe emotional and behavioural difficulties. Cole, Visser & Upton (1998) analysed over 80 Ofsted reports, then visited those schools identified as exemplars of good practice.

Head teachers from some of these schools were invited to joint the National Advisory Group which was established at Whitehall to draft new guidance specifically for those settings. The draft guidance was entitled 'Positive Handling Strategies for Pupils with Severe Behavioural Difficulties' (2001) and the consultation received a favourable response from schools.

Meanwhile the Department of Health had commissioned BILD to develop its own guidance provisionally entitled, 'Guidance on the Use of Restrictive Physical Interventions for Staff Working with Children and Adults who Display Extreme Behaviour in Association with Learning

Disability and/or Autistic Spectrum Disorders' (2001). The fact that the BILD guidance paid little attention to children with EBD was not a problem as this guidance had not been written for an EBD audience. It only became a problem when political considerations came to the fore. Having two government departments issuing guidance on the same subject was a problem. The latest catch phrase within government at the time was 'joined up thinking' and civil servants were under pressure to deliver some evidence that it meant something.

Political expedience carried the day as the DfES document, which had focused on emotional and behavioural difficulties, was quietly buried and substantially replaced by the DoH version, which had focused on severe learning disabilities. This was rushed through and trumpeted as the first example of joint guidance.

The DoH had invited BILD to draft the guidance on its behalf. The prevailing view seemed to be that training in physical intervention would only apply to a small number of specialist settings, such as those for severe learning difficulties and autism. For this reason BILD may have seemed to be the organisation with most experience.

Only at the last minute, were some sections of particular relevance to children with emotional and behavioural difficulties included.

However, there was growing evidence that mainstream schools needed training too. Carers of children and young people with emotional and behavioural difficulties, who represented a significant majority, were concerned that the focus was too narrow. Once again there had been a failure to appreciate the importance of context.

BILD resources were directed towards people with severe learning disability and autism. Other children and young people, who exhibited more deliberate challenging behaviour in both EBD and mainstream settings, were not their priority. But this form of challenging behaviour could not be ignored. Carers were already intervening in extremely challenging situations without relevant guidance, training or support. As late as 2002, the BILD accrediting panel was questioning the need for training in situations where pupils might use weapons.

In December 1995 Philip Lawrence, a London head teacher, had been stabbed to death outside his school by a 15 year old schoolboy as he heroically attempted to protect one of his pupils. Ignoring unpalatable truths does not make them go away.

Benefits of Training

Good behaviour management involves making skilled interventions at all stages of a potential crisis in order to steer away from aggression and violence. Training should promote an holistic approach, because positive physical interventions are not something separate from diffusion and de-escalation, they are part of the continuum of effective behaviour management strategies.

Some managers have argued against training staff in physical techniques, fearing that giving carers those skills would make them more likely to use them. The evidence suggests exactly the opposite.

In a review of the literature, Wright et al (2002) concluded that training in effective physical restraint skills had a significant impact on the ability of trainees to de-escalate, thus making it less likely that they would have to resort to physical interventions. Training in de-escalation alone did not have such a marked effect.

Why should it be that people trained in physical techniques should be better at de-escalating than people who are only trained in de-escalation? Allen et al (1997) reported the effects of improved staff confidence following training which equipped carers with safe and effective physical skills as part of an holistic approach. They too reported that improving staff skills reduced the use of physical interventions and the rate of injuries to staff and clients, possibly because it gave carers more confidence. When street robbers are shown video sequences of people walking down a street they agree on those they would choose as targets. The choice is not simply related to size. Some people look more confident and it may be that the confidence which results from good training changes the body language of carers making it less likely that they will provoke assaults.

Edwards (1999) also reported improved teamwork as a crucial difference in the performance of carers after they had been trained in effective physical interventions.

The best physical techniques are designed according to bio-mechanical principles to ensure only a natural range of movement. Training programmes should differentiate between intentional and non-intentional behaviours, with the stress always on the least intrusive of those interventions likely to be successful. A common theme of effective training is that all physical techniques should be designed to use the minimum force for the shortest time.

Holding on the Ground

Responsible training organisations ensure that they provide a sufficiently wide range of gradual and graded responses to cater for differences in age, size, development and levels of challenging behaviour so they can provide training relevant to the context of the particular service setting.

Policy makers should be honest about the elevated risks associated with some forms of extreme behaviour. Government guidance (2002), acknowledges that in some settings it may be necessary to hold a person on the ground. There are occasions when the risks associated with ineffective attempts to force a person to remain upright outweigh those associated with holding on the ground.

Blanket bans tend to be a simplistic response to a complex set of issues. A rational approach must balance the risks, and the risks associated with ad hoc responses will always outweigh those associated with good training.

There are safe and effective techniques which reduce risk in situations in which people are held on the ground, but they must be properly taught. Those who refuse to provide training, when they are aware that carers have been taken to the ground in the past, are not fulfilling their responsibilities either to the carers or the people they care for.

Particular attention should be paid to the possibility that some people may have suffered abuse in the past. Braise-Smith (1995) described women with mental health problems who had previously been the victims of rape. They reported flashbacks of sexual trauma and feelings such as domination, loss of dignity and vulnerability during physical interventions. Every effort should be made to avoid positions which are likely to trigger such responses.

For example, no techniques should allow people to be straddled on the ground. Every attempt should be made to maintain dignity for all concerned. Positional asphyxia has been associated with pressure applied to the torso in some ground restraint techniques in the past. Even minimal pressure on the torso can significantly restrict breathing. When a rotund person is held face down, with pressure on the torso, the stomach can be forced into the chest cavity preventing the lungs from expanding fully. When a violent person is expending energy during a restraint an oxygen debt can easily develop.

Health and Safety during Training

Risk can never be eliminated, but training providers should take all reasonable steps to reduce it as far as possible.

Providers of training have a duty of care to their course members, but participants should be reminded that they too have responsibilities for their own health and safety, and that of others on the course. In the operational situation it is always recommended that at least two members of staff should be available in a crisis situation, but the reality is that sometimes carers find themselves working alone. For that reason single person techniques should be included in the training framework. There should be no unannounced movements during initial training while techniques are being perfected and course members should be instructed not to offer resistance. Good training involves minimal force so that all course members can develop maximum technical proficiency in the limited time available. All practical exercises should be controlled, deliberate and accurate: not fast and furious.

Chapter 5 - Documenting

Duty of Care

The term 'duty of care' is an important legal term. Anyone who is paid to work with people for whom they have a responsibility has a duty of care towards them. Employers have a duty of care towards their staff and any other people who may use their premises. It would be negligent of an employer not to provide time and resources for proper training, but employees have a responsibility to look after themselves and the people around them. It would also be negligent of an employee not to access training when it was offered, or to read guidance which was readily available.

Negligence has three main elements. Firstly there must be a duty of care, secondly there must be a breach of that duty and thirdly, there must be some ensuing damage or injury related to the breach.

Reasonable

Our legal system hinges on the word 'reasonable' but the word keeps changing its meaning. A breach of duty of care could involve either taking unreasonable action, an act of commission, or failing to take reasonable action, an act of omission.

What is considered 'reasonable' depends largely upon what other people, with similar skills, knowledge and responsibilities would do in similar circumstances. One way to find out what other people are doing is to share ideas, look at other people's documentation and practice, be open and invite people in, try to visit other settings and attend conferences. Poor practice tends to develop when people become protective and isolated.

Case Law has established that carers must, 'Exhibit the responsible, mental qualities of a prudent parent in the circumstances of school life.' (Justice Edmund Davies Lyes v Middlesex County Council, 1962), and 'Take all reasonable and proper steps to protect the child,' (Justice Geoffrey Lane Beaumont v Surrey, 1968).

The Children Act 1989

The Children Act has been cited carelessly as the authority for a range of personal opinions about behaviour management and physical interventions, and as a result a number of carers faced allegations during the 1990s. In fact the The Children Act itself had very little to say on the matter.

Some organisations responded by introducing blanket bans on what were perceived as 'risky' activities. For example, managers in some child care settings introduced so-called 'no touch' policies. This approach was misconceived, because even those who pretended to have such policies were aware that they were not being followed. More importantly, they breached the first principle of The Children Act by placing the protection of staff above the best interests of the child. Regimes in which carers were told that they should not risk comforting a crying child or prevent one child from hurting another could reasonably be described as abusive.

Section 4, of the Children Act Guidance first addressed the issue of physical interventions in the context of Social Services children's homes. It was issued by the Department of Health and supplemented in 1993 by 'Permissible Forms of Control in Children's Residential Care.' According to some interpretations of this guidance, carers were not to take pro-active steps to prevent a child from coming to harm, but must wait until the risk was imminent, even if this reduced their ability to act effectively to protect the child.

Some interpreted 'significant injury' as meaning only life threatening physical injury, and argued that carers need not bother about such things as moral harm, access to drugs or criminal activities. There was also confusion about what constituted 'serious damage', resulting in some policies suggesting that carers should stand back and allow children to wreck their homes.

These interpretations represented a fundamental misunderstanding of the central tenet of The Children Act. In order to act in the best interests of the child, a professional carer is expected to act as a reasonable parent.

To correct some of these misunderstandings, a clarification was issued in February 1997, entitled, 'The Control of Children in the Public Care: Interpretation of the Children Act 1989. In this guidance Sir Herbert Laming, Chief Inspector at the Social Services Inspectorate, commented that sometimes 'the last resort' policy had looked 'suspiciously like an excuse for doing nothing.' He instructed Directors of Social Services in such authorities to change their policy.

Section 550A of the Education Act 1996

This outlined the powers teachers and other staff have to use reasonable force in schools. The Guidance which followed (10/98 in England and

37/98 in Wales) detailed the circumstances in which this was lawful. The politics of the time dictated that the power to authorise staff was given to head teachers rather than Local Education Authorities. This produced some anomalies, because many people who work with children are not directly employed by schools. Local Authorities retain responsibility for training their own staff, for example school escorts, although legally they cannot authorise them to act. Head teachers have the responsibility to identify all non-teaching staff who are authorized to use 'reasonable force' and they must keep an up-to-date list.

Amongst the carers who have been authorised under this legislation are classroom assistants, care workers, midday supervisors, specialist support assistants, personal assistants, escorts, caretakers, voluntary helpers, education welfare officers and mentors.

It follows that anyone who is authorised to make physical interventions should be trained in order to ensure they are competent and safe. Some local authorities have already implemented training for staff such as escorts involved in transport. Others have some way to go.

The Offences against the Person Act 1861

An assault may be committed if a person causes the apprehension in another that they may do harm. This could mean just raising a fist or issuing a verbal threat. Nobody needs to be injured, hurt or even touched for the technical offence to take place.

The offence of assault and battery may be committed if a person touches another without permission. They do not have to touch flesh for the offence to take place. Even to touch another person's clothing may be sufficient.

Restriction of Liberty

A civil offence of false imprisonment may be committed if a person is kept against their will, no matter whether any force is applied or not. It is sufficient that somebody intends to prevent the person from leaving of their own free will.

Getting Defensive

Common Law has an important place in our judicial system. It is based on precedence: the principle of deciding cases according to previous judicial decisions. According to precedent, if a person acts instinctively, in the heat of the moment and in good faith, this may form a justifiable common law defence. Professor Christina Lyon (2003) suggested that when physical interventions are used by carers, examples of a relevant defence would be when an individual takes reasonable steps to defend self, family or others from injury, or to prevent harm to another person or property.

It is difficult to negotiate crowded public transport systems without being placed in a position where somebody could make an allegation under the Offences against the Person Act. The accused person would need a reasonable defence, perhaps that it was an unavoidable accident. In a packed tube train this might be accepted. If a person walked over to another in an empty carriage and touched them, that would be more difficult to defend.

Open Cultures

It follows from this that simply trying to avoid any situation that may expose a member of staff to an allegation is not a viable strategy. It makes more sense to be clear about the 'lawful excuse' for any actions taken which may provide a reasonable defence.

Of course there are people who use the cover of forced proximity in a crowded train to commit offences. Similarly there are people who use the cover of professional care to get close to children and abuse them. That is why we need open, transparent and robust reporting procedures. If a member of staff accidentally touches another person or feels they have been placed in a compromising position, they should never pretend it has not happened. Carers should apologise if appropriate, report it as soon as possible and tell people what has happened immediately.

We need our child protection resources to focus on catching child abusers, not financing protracted investigations into genuine mistakes.

The United Nations Convention on the Rights of the Child

This was ratified by the UK government in 1991. As part of the provisions, the government undertook not only to promote children's rights but to actively ensure that children were made aware of them. This caused some alarm in education circles when it was suggested that signs should be placed in classrooms informing children that they had the right to leave any time they like, in order to avoid allegations of false imprisonment.

Children do have the right to leave a classroom, but the prevailing view at the time was that it would not be helpful to actively encourage pupils to exercise their rights in this area. In March 2003 it was reported that some schools had attempted to lock secondary pupils in their classrooms to prevent them from attending protests against the invasion of Iraq. Such actions would leave them open to legal challenge.

Human Rights Act 1998

Under the Human Rights Act, any actions involving restrictive physical interventions must be 'absolutely necessary'. The Act makes a presumption that everyone is born with rights and governments have a responsibility to ensure that their citizens are not prevented from enjoying those rights. Human rights include respect for private life, protection from inhuman or degrading treatment, liberty and security, and protection against discrimination.

If the actions of a carer could be construed as restricting the human rights of the person they are looking after, they need to demonstrate that those actions are absolutely necessary and in the best interests of the service user.

Special Educational Needs and Disability Act 2001

This legislation extended disability rights into education. The Act makes it unlawful to discriminate against pupils or prospective pupils who have a significant, long term mental or physical impairment. Long term is defined as lasting for more than one year. The legislation covers the whole life of the school including dinner breaks and school visits. Any form of less favourable treatment, for example preventing a pupil with behaviour difficulties from going on a school trip, would need to be justified. Under this legislation those with a duty to prevent discrimination are expected to anticipate what might put an individual at disadvantage and make 'reasonable adjustments' to their provision in order to avoid it. Breaches of this duty could result in a claim to the SEN and Disability tribunal. Reasonable adjustments include enhanced staffing levels, staff training and the drawing up of guidance for staff.

Health & Safety at Work Act 1974

A sensible risk reduction approach involves assessing risks, acknowledging where they exist and taking steps to reduce them. We cannot eliminate all risk; sometimes all we can do is balance one risk against another and choose the best possible option.

Risk assessment is probabilistic in nature, which means that we must accept that sometimes carers do the right thing, but still something goes wrong. When carers act in the best interests of a child or another person they deserve the support of management, no matter what the outcome.

Management of Health & Safety at Work Regulations 1992

This additional guidance stated that employers must provide supervision, instruction and training for their staff. They must also take responsibility for everyone at the workplace, including visitors and service users. A previous form of wording, 'so far as is reasonably practicable,' which allowed employers some flexibility, was replaced by an "absolute obligation irrespective of cost, time or inconvenience." Employers must provide a safe working environment and safe systems of work.

All workplaces should have written procedures for danger areas and emergencies, including risks of physical attack which could lead to injury. Human beings can be just as dangerous as faulty equipment, and the Health & Safety legislation gives people the right to be protected against such foreseeable risks. This applies to any environment in which a risk has been identified or can be anticipated. Any child who has previously injured another person represents a risk which can, and should, be anticipated.

Local Managers have a duty to introduce and maintain effective planning, organisation, control and monitoring arrangements.

Rights and Responsibilities

With rights come responsibilities. Employees also have a legal duty to take reasonable care of themselves and others who could be affected by what they do or don't do. They must co-operate with the employer to ensure that Health & Safety requirements are complied with. They must also report to their employer, or Health & Safety Adviser, any matter in which safety is compromised, and any shortcomings in the system.

The Welfare of the Child – The Best Interest Principle

Rather than becoming anxious about all the legal details, carers should focus on the first principle of the Children Act. The welfare of the child must be the paramount consideration in every decision which affects a child. Paramount means it is the first consideration and this takes precedence over all other considerations. This also reflects the best interest principle of the Human Rights Act.

If a member of staff acts honestly and in good faith to protect what they perceive to be the best interests of the child, this is the strongest defence for any action.

Standard 23 National Minimum Standards for Care Homes for Younger Adults

This is concerned with ensuring that service users are protected from abuse, neglect and self harm. Standard 23.5 requires that:

- Physical and verbal aggression by a service user in understood and dealt with appropriately
- Physical intervention is used only as a last resort by trained staff in accordance with Department of Health Guidance
- Physical intervention protects the rights and best interests of the service user and is the minimum consistent with safety."

Joint Guidance 2002

The first example of joint guidance from the Department of Health, and Department for Education and Skills was published in July 2002. In it, the term 'Restrictive Physical Interventions' replaced 'Physical Restraint.' However the guidance is clear that restrictive physical intervention does mean the use of force to control a person's behaviour.

'Restrictive Physical Interventions' are those which restrict movement, mobility or involve carers in disengaging from dangerous or harmful physical contact. In all actions the guidance reminds carers that the best interests of the service user are the paramount consideration. This reflects both The Children Act and the Human Rights Act.

Physical intervention should not be used to minimise disruption for staff. While it may be reasonable to withdraw a school pupil who is preventing other children from working, it would not be reasonable to strap a disruptive pupil with learning disability into a standing frame as a means of controlling behaviour.

Restrictive physical interventions should involve the minimum use of force for the shortest period of time. They should be designed to prevent injury, pain and distress and maintain the dignity of all involved. Any actions taken should be reasonable, proportionate and absolutely necessary.

Together, the Children Act 1989, Education Act 1996, Human Rights Act 1998 and the Health & Safety Act 1974 provide a clear framework under which professional carers are empowered to take positive action to control dangerous behaviour and protect the interests of children and adult service users. Where there are apparent contradictions in guidance, managers should follow the most recent interpretations.

Yet guidelines, no matter how good they may be, should be drawn upon discriminatingly. No guidelines can relieve staff of their primary responsibility, which is the welfare of those in their care. Carers are expected to think, to make considered judgements, and to ensure that any action they take is proportionate and reasonable, bearing in mind the particular circumstances. They should also be clear in their own minds about why it is absolutely necessary.

Recording and Reporting

Organisations need to have a policy in place to guide their staff so they know how to assess risk, formulate and implement plans to reduce risk and review their performance.

Employers and staff are judged on what they do and document. A policy framework may be described as having three layers:

- Policy principles contain generalisations which apply across a wide range of contexts.

- An organisational policy should relate those principles to the specific context in which they will be applied.

- Practice guidance should add sufficient detail to inform job descriptions.

People who have a history of challenging behaviour can present a risk under Health and Safety legislation. Where risk is foreseeable there is a legal requirement for a fully documented risk assessment to be put into place which both outlines the risk and details strategies to reduce the risk. It is good practice to maintain a record of who was involved in the formulation of the plan and who agreed to it. Everybody with a legitimate interest should be made aware of individual plans, including the person they apply to, and all incidents should be recorded to inform future reviews.

An unanticipated risk can only happen once. If any person has presented a risk in the past, then there should be an individual plan unless there is some reason to believe the risk has abated.

Policies

Policies should emphasise that all actions should be reasonable and proportionate. Under Human Rights legislation any actions taken which could be regarded as impeding a person's access to those rights must be absolutely necessary.

These phrases are important and should be used in all the relevant documentation. Similarly the language in policy documentation should reflect the most recent definitions, to avoid confusion. For example the 2002 joint guidance distinguishes between the terms, 'seclusion', 'time out' and 'withdrawal.'

- Seclusion involves forcing a person to remain alone in a room or building, either by locking them in or physically barring a door. It cannot be part of a planned response without a court order. Without a court order it would be difficult to justify other than in an extreme emergency.

- Time out is the withdrawal of reward as part of a behavioural therapy programme.

- Withdrawal involves moving a person to a safer place and remaining with them to supervise and support.

It is recommended that policy documents should explain clearly the circumstances in which any locked doors may be used and emphasise the need for adult supervision and support. The policy should quote the relevant section of the 2002 joint guidance, along with the 1997 clarification from the Department of Health.

The 2002 guidance advises that policy documents should be explicit about minimal discomfort which may be associated with some disengagement techniques. This should not be confused with techniques relying on the application of pain for compliance.

The concept of what is reasonable does not remain static, but is proportionate to the risk. This can be discussed with children, young people and adult service users who should be encouraged to contribute to the search for better ways of dealing with behaviour problems. Nobody should be under any doubt that the response expected from staff who find themselves being held is that they will apply the least intrusive, effective technique to disengage. The least intrusive technique is usually a verbal prompt, but failing this, mechanical disengagement is appropriate.

A policy which does not guide practice is worthless. The policy should clearly define areas of responsibility and authority. Every person issued with the policy should confirm that they have read and understood its contents by signing a record to that effect. When people realise they have to sign up to a policy they often decide to read it again just to check what they are agreeing to.

Individual Plans

Proactive strategies normally involve changing the environment and altering routines in order to reduce the risk of problems arising. They may include strategies to defuse and de-escalate, focusing on diversion, reassurance and communication.

Reactive strategies also need to be in place so that carers have the ability to respond in an emergency.

The first response is to prevent the situation from getting any worse and ensure safety. For some individuals, where it has been agreed that proactive use of restrictive physical intervention is in their best interests, this should be in the plan. For example, a child may have a series of rituals which indicate that behaviour is beginning to escalate. If it can be shown that taking early action reduces risk and prevents them from becoming more distressed or aggressive, then a proactive response is justified. This may involve withdrawing to a safer or less stimulating place. However, proactive interventions should always be part of a broader educational or therapeutic strategy and have a clear written rationale.

Individual plans should involve colleagues from various disciplines working together with the person, family and carers. These plans come under a variety of headings according to the service setting. Amongst these are Support and Intervention Plans, Individual Care Plans, Individual Behaviour Plans, Individual Education Plans and Positive Handling Plans.

Locked Doors

According to the most recent guidance high or double handles on doors may be used as a safety measure, and it is reasonable to lock outside doors or take other security measures. The key point is that children must be supervised by an adult whenever locked doors are used without specific statutory powers, and the policy should be explicit about this.

Who is Authorised and Trained

Those carers who are expected to use restrictive physical interventions, other than teachers, need written authorisation. Good practice suggests that a record should be kept of what training carers have had, who is trained to do what and when formal refresher training is due. The guidance states that staff should only use techniques with which they are confident and familiar.

Protective Recording

Good documentation protects both carers and those they care for. The DfES Guidance (April 2001) recommends that records should be both detailed and contemporaneous. A record should be made in a bound incident book with consecutively numbered pages. The incident should be recorded within 24 hours, preferably on the same day as it occurs. The record in the incident book could be cross referenced to more detailed incident sheets which may be kept elsewhere. A comprehensive recording system for serious incidents might include some of the following fields. Many of them could be tick boxes:

- Name of service user
- Day – Date – Time – Where it happened
- Name of person completing the form – printed and signed
- Names of all involved
- What led up to the incident
- Steps taken to avoid the incident (possibly in the form of a tick list)
    - Rights and Responsibilities Talk
    - Reassurance
    - Rules reminder
    - Choice Language
    - Assessment
    - Listening
    - Humour
    - Distraction
    - Withdrawal offered
    - Withdrawal directed
    - Making the environment safer
- A brief factual account of what exactly happened
- Was the behaviour -Deliberate? Reckless? Racial? Health & Safety Risk?
- Was the service user warned before any physical intervention?
- Was any holding 'mild' or 'firm'?
- Name the approved techniques used
- How effective was the intervention, including any problems with the technique?
- Length of contact in minutes
- Were airways, breathing and circulation monitored?

- Any injuries
- Contacts made
- How the incident was resolved
- What could we do differently next time?
- Evidence of debrief with service user
- Evidence of debrief with senior staff
- Has the Individual Plan been implemented or reviewed as a result of this incident?
- Is a further review date set?

Chapter 6 - Learning

"To move the world we must first move ourselves."

Socrates

Habitual therapy does not just apply to behaviour. People can become trapped by ineffective habitual mental responses when they are faced with a problem. Some people tend to reject new ideas in favour of familiar old ones, even if the old ideas have not worked in the past. They rehearse and reiterate old problems, rather than looking for new ideas and solutions. This pattern of thinking not only limits their own opportunities but sometimes pulls other people down too.

Habitual Blockers

"Our reach should exceed our grasp, or what's a heaven for?"

Robert Browning

Habitual blockers do not just fail to put forward constructive suggestions themselves, they tend to dismiss other people's ideas too. Even though they may not be aware of it, the habitual thinking exhibited by some staff members can corrupt a whole team. Habitual blockers search for reasons why new ideas might not work, rather than looking for ways to make them work. They will claim that it has all been tried before and failed. If such attitudes are allowed to prevail, they can soon stifle new ideas and trap organisations in a spiral of miserable failure. Habitual blockers and professional cynics cannot be allowed to dominate staff groups. The code of conduct for staff should include an expectation that all colleagues share the responsibility to raise morale, make positive suggestions, encourage others and make ideas work. Once this has been established and agreed, the behaviour of the habitual blocker and the professional cynic becomes either a capability or a disciplinary issue.

Habitual Movers

"Imagination is more important than knowledge."

Albert Einstein

A more positive approach is to recognise and acknowledge when a strategy is not working, then try something else. Effective people tend to

97

develop a range of habitual thinking responses which focus on moving forward towards solutions rather than blocking suggestions. In order to do this they have to be flexible in the way they think and respond. They listen carefully to the views of others and take time to think of ways to avoid stalemates and win/lose situations. They tend to act as if they are in control, even when they may not be feeling that confident. They are always looking for a better way of doing things. Effective team members do not try to deal with every situation themselves. They do not expect colleagues to cope without help either. But they do retain personal responsibility for problems and attempt to move them forward and follow them through to a conclusion, rather than passing them on for others to deal with.

In care settings effective people look forwards not backwards. They always respond to the first sign of acceptable behaviour, no matter what has happened before. They are paid to help people out of difficult situations, but it is also in the interests of carers to respond immediately to any positive behaviour, even if it is inconvenient at the time. The more often carers respond immediately to examples of positive behaviour, the greater the likelihood of positive behaviour being repeated. Often the problem with people who exhibit challenging behaviour is that they have learned that it works. As the opportunities to seize positive behaviour become rarer they become more valuable. We should never waste a valuable opportunity.

That is why carers should always welcome people back, accept apologies and seize any opportunity to solve a problem and move on, rather than prolong it over some perceived matter of principle.

Habitual movers maintain a sense of proportion and model good practice, which is picked up both by colleagues and the people they care for. They can be just as influential in a staff team in a positive way, as the habitual blockers and professional cynics can be in a negative way.

States of Mind

A state of mind involves both the way a person is feeling and the way they are thinking. When people are depressed, they tend to have negative thought patterns. As they rehearse negative thoughts they reinforce miserable feelings, and miserable brains tend to generate miserable thoughts. True clinical depression involves a chemical imbalance which may require drug therapy, but some people are just trapped in habitual patterns of thinking, feeling and behaving which keep them in a miserable loop. They find themselves in a bad mood, without really being aware of how it happened, and without any strategies for changing the situation. Learned helplessness is a state in which people are so crushed, they can no longer motivate themselves to do anything to change their circumstances. They become passive, resentful flotsam and jetsam, washed in and out by the tide of life.

Pessimists and Optimists

Pessimism and optimism are habitual states of mind. Pessimism gets a bad press but in some situations, where the cost of failure is extremely high, pessimism is an effective way of thinking. It prevents people from taking dangerous risks and making costly mistakes. However, most of the time, optimism has proved to be a far better strategy.

Some people think they were born lucky and others think the world is out to get them. Surprisingly they both share exactly the same habitual pattern of thinking. The three dimensions of this thinking are permanence, pervasiveness and personalisation.

What distinguishes a pessimist from an optimist is when they choose to apply this pattern of thinking. For example, when an event happens they will both sometimes choose to assume that the effects of it will be permanent, that they will pervade other areas of life and that whatever happened was personal; something to do with them.

The major difference is that optimists only apply this thought pattern when things go well. Optimists tend to forget the occasions when things go wrong. The optimist assumes that any setback is only temporary, the effects will be limited and whatever went wrong was not their fault. But when things go well, optimists claim the credit. When things go well optimists assume they will continue to go well. They assume that the positive benefits will be felt in other areas of their life and they take personal credit.

Pessimists apply the thinking pattern only when things go wrong. They tend to forget their successes. When something goes wrong they assume this is a sign of things to come, they convince themselves that the implications could be dire and affect other areas of their lives. They take it all personally, either blaming themselves or asking, 'Why me?'

These patterns of habitual thinking seem to be automatic, however, some people have chosen to change them. Of course, the habitual blockers will reject the notion of change and pessimists will want to convince themselves that it will not work. It takes an effort, but we do have a choice about how we feel.

Choice

The psychologist Mihaly Csikszentmihalyi, former professor at Chicago University, dedicated his career to the study of what makes people happy. He identified a key feature of human happiness as the need to feel in control of the events which shape our lives.

When people suffer from depression they often report a feeling of helplessness, and a loss of control. Stress is not just about the demands being made on a person, but the capacity of that person to control events and do something about it. The perception that people have choices and can influence the events which shape their lives both reduces stress levels and increases the endorphins in the brain that are associated with pleasure.

One way of influencing other people's feelings in a positive way is to create choices for them. This is particularly important for people who are looked after by others and who often have decisions made on their behalf, which can erode their perception of control and participation. For that reason it is important that an effort is made to allow participation in decision making at all levels. Nobody has unlimited choice and not everything is open to negotiation. However, opportunities can be created to allow people a limited range of options to choose from. Even when the options available are not open to negotiation, the timing and order of delivery could be. Ian Gilbert (2002) gives an example of creating choice to promote marital harmony. "Would you prefer me to go to the pub before dinner, or afterwards?"

Keeping Positive

"There is neither good nor bad but thinking makes it so."

Shakespeare

In some schools and care settings the ratio of directive or negative comments to positive ones can be unbalanced, sometimes with four directive comments to every positive one.

It takes a deliberate effort to reverse this damaging ratio, but the effects can be marked. Giving accurate feedback is important but there is no evidence that upsetting people has any beneficial effects. Honest feedback can be structured to keep the mood positive. The 'PIN' acronym stands for Positive, Interesting and Negative. It suggests the order in which feedback should be delivered. When providing feedback the carer should begin by talking about several things they like, moving on to interesting features, before finally referring to any negative aspect and suggesting how it can be improved.

Keep Smiling

Smiling may be a good habitual behaviour to develop. Smiling triggers an automatic response in other people, causing them to smile in return. It also makes other people feel subconsciously better disposed towards the person who is smiling. It communicates confidence and openness.

Treats

Treats can have a positive effect, especially if they are unexpected. These are not the same as the contingent rewards used to train animals to perform a range of impressive tricks. For example, when dolphins are being taught to leap through hoops, the trainer may begin by throwing a fish as the dolphin swims near the surface. As it swims near the bottom of the pool there is no fish. The next time the Dolphin happens to move towards the surface the trainer throws another fish, and so on. Gradually the dolphin begins to swim up to the surface more often and is soon leaping out of the water through hoops. This is called behaviour shaping through contingent rewards.

Treats are not a reward for doing anything in particular. They are a deliberate attempt to change the mood. Sometimes even dolphins seem to lose interest and stop playing. Experienced trainers abandon conditional rewards when the dolphins lose interest. They may take a break then throw a whole bucket of fish into the pool.

This unexpected treat changes the mood in the pool and the dolphins start playing again, so the behaviour shaping can resume. There is a place for random unexpected treats in every environment, especially when the communal mood has become blocked.

Fear of Failure

"To change one's life: Start immediately. Do it flamboyantly. No exceptions!"

William James

Some people are disabled by the fear of failure, which prevents them from taking risks when they are presented with opportunities to learn new skills or form new relationships. People who have been hurt in the past when they tried something new, learn not to risk failure. Instead of feeling excited at the prospect of a new opportunity or a new relationship they experience anxiety at the threat of being hurt or humiliated once more. Some children, especially those in the care system have been repeatedly failed, hurt and humiliated. They find it increasingly difficult to commit to a new relationship. Instead, they test new relationships to destruction, or sabotage their attempts to learn a new skill, creating a self fulfilling prophesy and reinforcing their suspicions of new people and new things.

When an experience has been painful in the past, people respond to similar situations with anxiety. That is why disturbed children often respond to judgemental praise by destroying the piece of work being praised.

Inducing Moods

Experiments have shown that encouraging people to recall or relate unpleasant, or painful, experiences induces dramatic and sustained negative mood changes. Even thinking about imaginary situations can bring about measurable physiological changes. In one experiment people were told to imagine their partner being unfaithful. Their skin conductivity, a measure of stress, increased measurably as did the involuntary contraction of the corrugator muscles in the brow, even though they were not aware of it.

This is a good reason to avoid forms of therapy which encourage people to relive past traumas. In spite of their popularity there is absolutely no research evidence that they have any beneficial affects whatsoever, in spite of numerous attempts to prove some benefits. Recent long term studies of the survivors of World Trade Centre attacks in New York confirm that those who received this form of counselling from professional therapists were more traumatised after a year than people who had received no counselling at all.

Guided Imagery

People can be guided towards more positive emotions instead. Guided imagery is a technique which can introduce pronounced positive changes in the way a person feels.

The technique involves asking a person to remember or imagine that they are in their favourite place, or recall the best day of their lives. By mentally adding sounds, colours and smells the image can be made stronger and the feelings evoked more powerful. This exercise can bring about positive mood change, but only if the person can be persuaded to try out the exercise.

Like all other forms of exercise, mental gymnastics takes effort and practice. It is not enough just to join the gym, you have to go and do some work. By practising and working on the positive image, people can create a tool to help them change the way they feel when they are under pressure.

Scream Savers

If thinking about one thing makes you feel bad, it makes sense to think about something else, but that is easier said than done. Telling people not to think about something is no help at all because it guides them in the wrong direction. You need something else to think about. What people need is a strong positive image which can be brought to mind to replace the unwanted thoughts.

Some people use breathing exercises as a relaxation technique and they can be made even more effective when combined with a well developed positive image. As the person brings the positive image to mind, they breathe in counting to three, hold the breath for a count of three, and then breathe out slowly for a count of six.

Each time the image is brought to mind it can be strengthened by building in more detail from all the senses. When people add colours, sounds, tastes, smells and feelings to a favourite memory it can become extremely vivid. Once this strong relaxing image has been practised, it can become a default 'scream saver.'

Just as the scream saver can be strengthened by adding detail from all the senses, similar techniques can be used in reverse to reduce the impact of recurrent thoughts which cause distress. One way to reduce the impact of a persistent worry is to help the person to imagine they are directing a film. They can imagine that they are pulling the shot back to make the distressing scene appear more distant and less threatening. They can blur the detail, take out the colour, degrade the sound and speed up the action. These techniques can enable people who are controlled by their moods to begin to feel more in control. Then they can turn to their favourite positive image instead.

Some people create a fantasy 'scream saver' by adding pleasurable details. It need not be true. It just needs to work.

Mood Resources

It makes sense to build up a collection of books, music and videos that put people into a good mood. If polishing up happy memories improves the way people feel then it might be a good idea to encourage people to keep photographs, audio and video recordings of positive experiences. Physical exercise is a proven method of changing the way people feel. It stimulates the production of endorphins. Just raising the arms in the air can increase the blood flow to the brain. Sometimes a change of scenery helps too. It makes sense to encourage physical exercise and invest in the equipment which encourages people to do it.

People have to be encouraged to do something, rather than just sitting and wondering why they are not feeling better.

Goal Setting

"No matter how hard the past, you can always begin again today."

Buddha

Some people drift through their lives, resenting the fact that nothing good ever happens to them. But waiting for your talents to be discovered is a poor life strategy. Successful people share the same attitude. They know where they want to be and start moving towards their goal. Talent is not always necessary.

Some famous people have claimed in their success was down to luck, but the golfer Gary Player noted that the more he practised the luckier he seemed to get. Positive attitudes, good social skills and hard work make luck happen.

Most successful people began by knowing what they wanted. Having goals gives people a direction. We can only tell if we are getting closer or further away from our destination if we know where we are supposed to be going. At the end of each day, if we have moved towards our goal, no matter how small the step, then the day has been a success.

This is a successful form of habitual thinking for everyone. People can model and teach effective thinking by talking about the way they think and make decisions.

There is no question that events shape our lives and change the way we feel and behave. Yet, for many people the events in their lives are not the major determinant of how they feel. Changing the way people habitually think changes the way they perceive and respond to events. There is abundant evidence that helping people to change habitual patterns of thinking and behaving can improve their lives. That is what changing minds is all about.

References
1. Allen B – 1992 - The Children Act Up - London: Lucky Duck Publications
2. Allen B – 1994 - Children In Control - London: Lucky Duck Publications
3. Allen B – 1994 - If It Makes My Life Easier – Behaviour Policies - London: Lucky Duck Publications
4. Allen B – 1998 - Holding Back – Restraint Rarely & Safely - London: Lucky Duck Publications
5. Allen B – 1998 - Holding Back – Video Training Pack - London: Lucky Duck Publishing
6. Allen B – 1998 - New Guidance On The Use Of Reasonable Force In Schools - British Journal of Special Education 25 4 p184-188
7. Allen B – 1999 - Emotional and Behavioural Difficulties: Unit 4 Management Of Aggression - Birmingham University Distance Learning Course
8. Allen B – 1999 - Conflict Management - In Visser J & Rayner S Editors Emotional and Behavioural Difficulties: A Reader Lichfield Qed Publications
9. Allen D McDonald A Dunn C & Doyle T – 1997 - Changing Care Staff Approaches To The Prevention And Management Of Aggressive Behaviour In A Residential Treatment Unit For Persons With Mental Retardation And Challenging Behaviour - Research in Developmental Disabilities 18 101-112
10. Allen D – 2001 - Training Carers In Physical Interventions: Research Towards Evidence Based Practice - BILD Publications
11. Anderson C A & Bushman B J – 2002 - Human Aggression - Annual Review of Psychology 2002 53: 27-51
12. Aunger R – 2002 - The Electric Meme: A New Theory Of How We Think - New York Free Press 2002
13. Arnett A & Hewett D – 1996 - 'Guidance On The Use Of Physical Force By Staff In Educational Establishments' - British Journal of Special Education Volume 23 No 3
14. Argyle M – 1988 - Bodily Communication 2nd Edition - London: Methuen
15. Barclay G Travers T & Siddiqui A – 2001 - International Comparisons In Criminal Justice Statistics 1999 - London: HMSO
16. Barkow J h Cosmides L & Tooby J – 1992 - The Adapted Mind: Evolutionary Psychology And The Generation Of Culture New York: Oxford University Press

17. Bamforth D B – 1994 - Indigenous People Indigenous Violence: Pre-Contact Warfare On The North American Great Plains - Man 29 95-115

18. Blackmore S – 1999 - The Meme Machine - Oxford University Press 1999

19. Blum D – 1997 - Sex On The Brain: The Biological Differences Between Men And Women - New York: Viking

20. Brase-Smith – 1995 - Restraints: Retraumatization For Rape Victims? - Journal of Psychosocial Nursing 33 23-28

21. British Institute of Learning Disabilities – 1996 - Physical Interventions: A Policy Framework - BILD Publications

22. British Institute of Learning Disabilities – 2002 - Easy Guide To Physical Interventions For People With Learning Disabilities Their Carers And Supporters - BILD Publications

23. British Institute of Learning Disabilities – 2002 - Good Practice In Physical Interventions - BILD Publications

24. Brookes M – 1998 - Control And Restraint Techniques: A Study Into Its Effectiveness At HMP Gartree Psychological Services Report Series 2 No 156 - London: Home Office Prison Department

25. Bushman B J Baumeister R F & Stack A – 1999 - Catharsis Aggression And Persuasive Influence: Self Fulfilling Or Self Defeating Prophecies? Journal of Personality and Social Psychology 76 (3) 367-376

26. Bushman B J & Baumeister R F – 1998 - Threatened Egotism Narcissism Self-Esteem And Direct And Displaced Aggression: Does Self-Love Or Self-Hate Lead To Violence? - Journal of Personality and Social Psychology 75 219-229

27. Bushman B – 2002 - Does Venting Anger Feed Or Extinguish The Flame? Catharsis Rumination Distraction Anger and Aggressive Responding Personality and Social Psychology Bulletin Vol 28 No 6 724-731

28. Bushman B J & Anderson C A – 2002 - Media Violence And The American Public: Scientific Facts Versus Media Misinformation - American Psychologist Association Vol 56 No 6/7 477-489

29. Bushman B J Bonacci A M van Dijk M & Baumeister R M – 2003 - Narcissism Sexual Refusal And Aggression: Testing A Narcissistic Reactance Model Of Sexual Coercion *Journal of Personality and Social Psychology*

30. Carmel H & Hunter M – 1989 - Staff Injuries From Inpatient Violence - Hospital & Community Psychiatry 40 41-46

31. Carmel H & Hunter M - 1990a - Compliance With Training In Managing Assaultive Behaviour And Injuries From Inpatient Violence - Bulletin of the American Academy of Psychiatry & The Law 21 485-493
32. Carmel H & Hunter M – 1993 - Staff Injuries From Patient Attack: Five Years Data Reducing Staff Injuries - Hospital & Community Psychiatry 40 41-46
33. Ciarrochi J Forgas J & Mayer J D (Eds) – 2001 - Emotional Intelligence In Everyday Life - New York: Psychology Press
34. Csikszentmihalyi M – 1993 - The Evolving Self - New York: Harper Collins
35. Cole T Visser J & Upton G – 1998 - Effective Schooling For Pupils With Emotional And Behavioural Difficulties - London: David Fulton Publishers
36. Davies W Frude N – 1993 - Preventing Face To Face Violence: Dealing With Anger And Aggression At Work - New York: APT
37. Damasio A – 2000 - The Feeling Of What Happens: Body Emotion And The Making Of Consciousness - London: William Heinneman Random House
38. Dawkins R - 1974/1998 - The Selfish Gene New Edition - New York: Oxford University Press
39. Delgado J – 1966 - Physical Control Of The Mind: Towards A Civilized Psychocivilised Society - New York: Harper Row
40. Dennett D C - 1991 - Consciousness Explained - Boston: Little Brown
41. Decartes R - 1637/2001R - Discourse On Method - New York: Bartleby Com
42. Department of Education and Science – 1988 - Discipline In Schools: Report Of The Committee Of Enquiry   London: H M S O
43. Department of Health – 1990 - Children In The Public Care: A Review Of Residential Care - London: H M S O
44. Department of Health – 1990 - The Care Of Children Principles And Practice In Guidance And Regulations - London: H M S O
45. Department of Health – 1991 - The Children Act 1989 Guidance And Regulations Volume 4 Residential Care - London: H M S O
46. Department of Health – 1991 - The Children Act 1989 Guidance And Regulations Volume 5 Independent Schools - London: H M S O

47. Department of Health – 1991 - Statutory Instruments 1991 No 1506 Children And Young Persons Children's Homes Regulations - London: H M S O

48. Department of Health – 1993 – 'Guidance On Permissible Forms Of Control In Children's Residential Care' - London: H M S O

49. Department of Health – 1997 - 'The Control Of Children In The Public Care: Interpretation Of The Children Act 1989' - London: H M S O

50. Department for Education & Employment – 1998 - 'Guidance On Section 550A Of The Education Act 1996: The Use Of Reasonable Force To Control Or Restrain Pupils' - London: H M S O

51. Department for Education & Employment – 2000 - Consultation On Positive Handling Strategies For Pupils With Severe Behavioural Difficulties - London: DfEE Draft Guidance

52. Department for Education & Employment – 2001 - 'Promoting Positive Handling Strategies - Letter and accompanying guidance sent from Chris Wells Head of SEN Division to Chief Education Officers

53. Department for Education and Skills – 2002 - Guidance On The Use Of Restrictive Physical Interventions For Staff Working With Children And Adults Who Display Extreme Behaviour In Association With Learning Disability And/Or Autistic Spectrum Disorders - London: Department for Education and Skills

54. Department of Health – 2002 - Guidance For Restrictive Physical Interventions: How To Provide Safe Services For People With Learning Disabilities And Autistic Spectrum Disorder   London: Department of Health

55. Edwards R – 1999 - The Laying On Of Hands: Nursing Staff Talk About Physical Restraint - Journal of Learning Disabilities for Nursing Health and Social Care 3 (3) 136-143

56. Ekman P (Editor) – 1998 - Ekman P (Editor) Charles Darwin's The Expression Of The Emotions In Man And Animals Third Edition With Introduction Afterwords And Commentaries By Paul Ekman - London: HarperCollins and New York: Oxford University Press 1998

57. Emler N – 2001 - Self Esteem: The Costs And Causes - Joseph Rountree Foundation

58. Forgas J P – 1995 - Mood And Judgment: The Affect Infusion Model - Psychological Bulletin 117 39-66

59. Freedman J L – 2002 - Media Violence And Aggression: No Evidence For A Connection - Toronto: University of Toronto Press
60. Gardner H – 1983 - Frames Of Mind: The Theory Of Multiple Intelligences - `New York: Basic Books
61. Gardner H – 1999 - Intelligence Reframed: Multiple Intelligences For The 21 Century - `New York: Basic Books
62. Gazzaniga M S – 1992 - Nature's Mind: The Biological Roots Of Thinking Emotions Sexuality Language and Intelligence - New York: Basic Books
63. Gilbert I – 2002 - Essential Motivation In The Classroom London: Routledge Falmer
64. Goldman D – 1995 - Emotional Intelligence: Why It Can Matter More Than IQ - New York: Bantham
65. Green R G & Quanty M B – 1977 - The Catharsis Of Aggression: An Evaluation Of A Hypothesis - In Berkowitz L (ed) Advances in Experimental Social Psychology (Vo 10 pp 1-37 New York: Academic Press
66. Harris J – 1996 - Physical Restraint Procedures For Managing Challenging Behaviours Presented By Mentally Retarded Adults And Children - Research in Development Disabilities 17 (2) 99-134
67. Harris J – 2001 - Physical Interventions – From Policy To Practice - The Journal of Adult Protection May 2001 Vol 3 Issue 2 18-24
68. Health and Safety Executive – 1989 - Violence To Staff - London: H M S O
69. Health & Safety Advisory Committee 1990 - Violence To Staff In The Education Sector - London: H M S O
70. Health and Safety Executive – 1994 - Essentials Of Health And Safety At Work   London: H M S O
71. Holden C - 1989 - The Genetics Of Personality - Science 237 598-601
72. Jensen A – 1972 - Genetics And Education - New York: Harper and Row
73. Kaplan S G & Wheeler E G – 1983 - Survival Skills For Working With Potentially Violent Clients - Social Casework 64 339-345
74. Kenrick D & Sheets V – 1994 - `Homicide Fantasies - Ethology and Sociobiology 14 231-246
75. King and Motulsky – 2002 - Human Genetics: Mapping Human History Science 2002 298: 2342-2343

76. Lyon C – 1994 - Legal Issues Arising From The Care Control And Safety Of Children With Learning Disabilities Who Also Present Severe Challenging Behaviour - London: Mental Health Foundation
77. Lyon C – 2003 – Legal Issues Arising from the Care and Control of Children, Young People and Adults with Learning Disabilities Presenting Severe Challenging Behaviour – Draft update produced for BILD
78. Maines B Robinson G - 2001 (New ed) - You Can...You Know You Can - Bristol: Lucky Duck Publishing
79. Mayer J D Salovey P Caruso D R & Sitarenios G – 2001 - Emotional Intelligence As A Standard Intelligence - Emotion 1 232-242
80. McDonnell A Dearden B & Richens A – 1991 - Staff Training In The Management Of Violence And Aggression 3 Physical Restraint - Mental Handicap 19 (151-154) 148-172
81. McGuinness D – 1997 - Why Our Children Can't Read - New York: Free Press
82. Mealey L Daood C & Frage M – 1996 - Enhanced Memory For Faces Of Cheaters - Ethology and Sociobiology 17 119-128
83. Mesquida C G & Wiener N I – 1996 - Human Collective Aggression: A Behavioural Ecological Perspective - Ethology and Sociobiology 17 247-262
84. Miller E K – 2000 - The Prefrontal Cortex And Cognitive Control - Nature Reviews Neuroscience 1 59-65
85. National Society for the Prevention of Cruelty to Children – 1990 - Violence: Staff Handbook - London: NSPCC Publications
86. Nind M & Hewett D – 2001 - A Practical Guide To Intensive Interaction - BILD Publications
87. Paterson B & McCornish S – 1998 - The Physical Management Of Violent Behaviour - Psychiatric Care 5 228-231
88. Phillips D & Rudestram K E – 1995 - Effect Of Nonviolent Self-Defence Training On Male Psychiatric Staff Members Aggression And Fear - Psychiatric Services 46 164-168
89. Pinker S – 2002 - The Blank Slate - London: Allen Lane
90. Pinker S – 1997 - How The Mind Works - New York: Norton
91. Pinker S – 1994 - The Language Instinct - New York: Harper Collins
92. Sperry R W – 1969 - A Modified Concept Of Consciousness - Psychological Review 1969 vol 76 no 6 p 532-536

93. Plomin R Owen M J & McGuffin P – 1994 - The Genetic Basis Of Complex Human Behaviours - Science 264 1733-1739
94. Raplin I – 2001 - An 8 Year Old Boy With Autism - Journal of the American Medical Association 285 1749-1757
95. Renfew J W – 1997 - Aggression And Its Causes: A Biopsychosocial Approach - New York: Oxford University Press
96. Skinner B F – 1974 - About Behaviourism - New York: Knopf
97. Salovey P & Mayer J D – 1990 - Emotional Intelligence - Imagination Cognition and Personality 9 185-211
98. Sperry R W Gazzaniga M S and Bogen J B – 1969 - Interhemispheric Relationships: The Neocortical Commissures; Syndromes Of Hemisphere Disconnection
99. In: P J Vinken and G W Bruyn Eds Handbook Clin Neurol 4 273-290
100. Tinbergen N 1952 - Derived Activities: Their Causation Biological Significance Origin And Emancipation During Evolution - Quarterly Review of Biology 27 1032
101. Turkheimer E – 2000 - Three Laws Of Behavior Genetics And What They Mean - Current Directions in Psychological Science 5 160-164
102. Webster R – 1995 - Why Freud Was Wrong - London: HarperCollins
103. Wheldall Kk & Merrett F – 1988 - More Sticks Than Carrots - Teachers Weekly 9 May
104. Wright S Gray R Parkes J & Gournay K – 2002 - The Recognition Prevention And Therapeutic Management Of Violence In Acute In -Patient Psychiatry: A Literature Review And Evidence-Based Recommendations For Good Practice - Report for UKCC: London
105. Zimbardo P G Maslach C & Haney C – 2000 - Reflections On The Stanford Prison Experiment: Genesis Transformations Consequences In T Blass Ed Current perspectives on the Milgram paradigm Mahwah H J : Erlbaum